The
Traditional Working Terrier

The Traditional Working Terrier

Seán Frain

SWAN·HILL
PRESS

Copyright © 2001 Seán Frain

First published in the UK in 2001
by Swan Hill Press, an imprint of Quiller Publishing Ltd

Reprinted 2003, 2007

British Library Cataloguing-in-Publication Data
A catalogue record for this book
is available from the British Library

ISBN 978 1 84037 308 0

The information in this book is true and complete to the best of our knowledge. All recommendations are made without any guarantee on the part of the Publisher, who also disclaims any liability incurred in connection with the use of this data or specific details.

Typeset by Phoenix Typesetting, Ilkley, West Yorkshire
Printed in England by MPG Books Ltd, Bodmin, Cornwall.

Swan Hill Press

an imprint of Quiller Publishing Ltd
Wykey House, Wykey, Shrewsbury, SY4 1JA, England
E-mail: info@quillerbooks.com
Website: www.countrybooksdirect.com

Dedicated to Mum and Dad,
for putting up with both me and my menagerie.

Acknowledgements

Thanks must go to *The Countryman's Weekly* for their assistance with Chapter 8, and especially to Brian Plummer who gave me much-needed advice and has supported my writing. Also to all those I have accompanied out in the open field for the past two decades. Thanks to all the farmers who allowed me to help out on their farms, and who taught me much about the countryside and showed me why pest control is an essential part of both making a living and managing our beautiful countryside – long may it be protected from the developers!

Contents

Introduction

'There the fly fox the careless minute waits,' wrote John Dyer (1699–1757) in his pastoral poem 'The New Dropp'd Lamb', well expressing the opportunism of the fox, efficient and ruthless in his endeavours. The poet John Fletcher also warns shepherds of the ever-present danger to their flocks in 'The Falling Night', saying:

> Let your dogs loose without,
> Lest the wolf come as a scout
> From the mountain and, ere day,
> Bear a lamb or kid away,
> Or the crafty, theivish fox,
> Break upon your simple flocks.

John Fletcher lived from 1579–1625, when the wolf was still a threat to a shepherd's livelihood, a threat now long gone, but it has to be remembered that the fox still remains a threat to a flock full of lambs during spring, and a very real danger to any farmers livestock, including chickens, ducks, geese and piglets, for Reynard is an expert hunter and can cause havoc wherever these animals are kept, especially for commercial reasons. I know of three people who have given up keeping chickens and ducks simply because raiding foxes have had a devastating effect upon their livestock numbers, and several others who are plagued by foxes taking their stock, but carry on undaunted.

If you talk to the hardy shepherds of the hill country, as I have, whether it be in Wales, Lancashire, Yorkshire, Cumbria or even Scotland, you will soon come to appreciate the accuracy of the words of the above poems. Try a spot of stock-keeping for yourself and I am certain that you will come to appreciate them even more!

Life has become so much easier in many ways during this century. We can pop out to the supermarket and do a full weekly shop, filling our trollies with all sorts of goodies, including meat, fruit and vegetables. We pay our money and away we go to stock up our cupboards, fridges and freezers, and we can even put a ready-made meal in a microwave oven and sit down to eat it within minutes of doing so – convenience shopping, convenience cooking, anything inconvenient done away with.

But it was not always like this! At one time, in better times some might say, most folk would grow a lot of their own vegetables and keep a small amount of livestock such as a pig or two, a cow, a few chickens etc, mainly for their own use, for few could afford to buy produce from someone else on a regular basis. These people really felt it if a fox got in among their stock and slaughtered several chickens or stole a piglet or two. Of course, foxes cannot raid our cupboards, fridges and freezers and so to most people today Reynard poses no threat whatsoever to their comfort but, it must not be forgotten that he does remain a threat to those who are now struggling to make a living on the farms of Britain and abroad. Even allotment holders on the edge of towns and cities can be plagued by them.

It is therefore easy to understand why, in Elizabethan times, a bounty of 2s. 6d. (12½p) was offered for the head of every fox accounted for, and why, when a fox was located in a wood or inside an earth during the times of the famous hunting parson John Russell, nearly the whole village turned out to deal with it. In fact, Russell had many a run-in with hardy Devonshire villagers intent on a little fox killing, for foxes had become scarce due to their forays with the local livestock and Russell believed that control, balanced with conservation, was the real job of the hunt and although it is true that providing sport was also a reason, it is possibly the main one. And where hunting was allowed for the control of this cunning predator, foxes thrived, their numbers steadily increasing as they recovered from persecution at the hands of those who would kill every fox they came across – a situation that could develop again if hunting with hounds is stopped!

Hunting foxes with hounds serves several different purposes, but the main reason for it – and a very good reason – is to control numbers. The rural community needs to provide protection for farmers and shepherds, not to mention smallholders who have a hard time of it in our modern world, which is systematically killing off so many of our traditional skills and pastimes.

Put yourself in the farmer's position for a moment. You inspect your stock in the grey dawn and you discover a lamb lying dead on the cold, wet grass, its head bitten off. You failed to get all your hens in last night and several of them now lie dead, while only one is missing. A piglet has gone, or maybe two, the sow too slow to protect it. What do you do? Cut your losses and carry on as though nothing has happened? If you follow this option, the fox will be back, or will pay someone else a visit before long, teaching its cubs this method of easier hunting. Alternatively you could call out the local hunt, whose well trained and disciplined hounds will pick up the scent of the culprit, track it to where it lies and dispatch it speedily.

Hunting with hounds provides an essential service for those who struggle to make a living in our beautiful countryside, and it is fair to say that this form of fox control would be nigh on impossible if it were not for the essential back-up provided by the humble little terrier which contributes greatly to the efficiency at which a pack operates – although it is also fair to say that terriers are often ignored by some quarters of the hunting world. But where it is impossible for control to be carried out by hounds, such as near busy roads, the terrier-lads can be called upon to deal with the foxes.

It is the humble little terrier, the gallant terrier, that is the subject of this publication and I hope to highlight its worth in carrying out effective fox control, as well as its charming character, which makes it an ideal member of the family, not just a working dog. For the terrier is a versatile creature that makes a true friend to all those who seek its companionship.

After a hard day working three foxes.

1

Terriers in History

Throughout the many centuries, right down to our day, dogs have been used for a large variety of tasks. They have been widely used for guarding and herding, as messengers, in war and for fighting each other and other animals (and sometimes even men); they were once commonly used for turning millstones in such places as Scotland and Wales, and in our day we see them helping the deaf and the blind, and sniffing out drugs. But the most common task for which dogs have been used must be hunting. Even the ancient Egyptians made use of dogs for hunting, as many carvings on temple walls testify. Saluki and Afghan types were extensively used for sight-hunting on the desert plains of this region, and greyhound types were also used for this purpose. And it appears that terrier types also originated from this area. A dachshund-type dog known as the Egyptian house dog was common in Egypt, and it seems that this dog, which was a little leggier and more powerfully built than the modern dachshund, may have been the ancestor of our modern terrier breeds. Later the Egyptians were also breeding small, long-haired terrier types which might have been the ancestors of the Maltese terrier types which are still to be seen today. It seems that Egyptian women were very fond of these dogs and kept them as companions and pets; whether they were used for any kind of hunting is unknown, though it is very likely.

Other breeds which were bred and hunted by the ancient Egyptians were the hound types and powerful, fearless mastiffs that were a key element in the development of terrier strains, as we shall see. Mastiffs were then all-round working dogs which could be used for a variety of tasks. First and foremost they were expert hunting dogs, but the Egyptians also used them for guarding and herding, and possibly as war dogs too. Other nations also found them very useful indeed; the Assyrians certainly made good use of them. They were very effectively used in war especially and no doubt the Assyrians enjoyed seeing these powerful dogs pulling down their enemies and their horses, thus satisfying some of this extremely cruel people's appetite for spilling blood. The Assyrians also used them for hunting in packs against wild horses and other animals. At this time the mastiff could hunt just as well by scent as it could by sight. I suspect that at some time these mastiffs entered the blood-lines of early hounds similar to those found in Egypt, and gave rise to the foundation stock of the hounds of today. The mastiff, it seems, was used not only in its own right as a breed, but also to create and develop other strains.

At that time, in those harsh desert regions and fertile valley plains, the principal means of livelihood was the raising and tending of sheep. The shepherd of today has to worry about foxes and rogue badgers, but in those days shepherds had a great deal more to worry about, for their flocks were in great danger from marauding lions and bears as well as smaller predators. It is therefore only logical that they turned to dogs to help them care for and protect their flocks. Mastiffs did the job well enough, but this fearless breed probably tackled lions and bears head-on, taking fearful maulings and most were probably killed. It seems likely therefore that the shepherds crossed them with more docile, sensible breeds which would still tackle predators but at the same time have the sense to stand back when the intruder retaliated. There were basenji-type dogs and other, more mongrel types, so it is possible that breeds such as these were mated with mastiffs and so specialist herding dogs began to be bred. The Persian herding dog was very powerful and obviously had mastiff ancestors, but other breeds had also gone into the mix. These herding dogs were popular amongst the shepherds of that time.

We can surmise that from these basic breeds which were common in the ancient world came all other breeds in one way or another, although it would be impossible to explain exactly how this occurred. Nevertheless I believe it is indisputable that our modern terrier breeds are descended from these dachshund and Maltese terrier types. But how did this happen when those ancient breeds were used halfway around the world? The answer lies in a small seaport on the Mediterranean.

The Phoenicians inhabited the region between Syria and Israel, up to the Lebanon mountains, and it is here that the small but very important seaport of Sidon could be found. the Phoenician people (the Canaanites of the Bible) were apparently very wicked, and were eventually destroyed because of their sins. But they were also expert shipbuilders whose vessels, unlike most others of the time, were easily capable of long sea journeys. These people soon became very important traders and trade routes were opened up to Sidon, and later Tyre, from many different places. One of the most popular trade routes passed through Assyria so, along with foodstuffs and other materials, dogs such as mastiffs, greyhounds, herding dogs, early hounds and terrier types were taken along these trade routes and then carried by the Phoenician traders over the sea to other countries. The Phoenicians did much trade with Egypt and no doubt those old Egyptian breeds also found their way onto cargo vessels, starting their long journey to many European countries, especially Spain and Greece, where the strains continued, and other breeds were created.

The Phoenicians were leaders in the sea trade, but it was not long before other races were following their example. Thus, when ships full of precious cargo sailed into the ports of other countries, the dogs they took with them mated with native dogs and so even more breeds were created. This Phoenician link is, I believe, just one of what I call the four keys which opened the doors for new breeds to be created and existing ones developed. It opened the door to many parts of Europe; the second key helped in spreading these breeds still further.

Spanish- and Greek-type terriers became rather popular in Europe, as did small hound types similar to the dachshund and basset of today. The Celts, a very powerful people, began to advance over most of Europe probably around the time when the traders from over the sea were doing business with Spain and other countries. These people were fierce and rather unruly, but they were great hunters who made good use of the dogs which were then available to them. Plato, writing in the fourth century BC, described the Celts as 'drink-loving war mongers', Aristotle wrote that they 'scorned danger', and Ptolemy, writing in the second century AD, said that they were 'a fearless people'. If the people themselves were fearless, then so were the dogs they used, no doubt in war, but also to hunt, wolves, wild boars and other animals. It is just possible that these Celtic people used hounds for hunting that were descended from mastiff breeds, or maybe the Persian molossus, which was related to the mastiff used by the Assyrians for a number of different tasks. Smaller hound types were possibly also used, as was a small corgi-like terrier that we know was being bred by the Celts as long as 3,000 years ago and which is said to be the ancestor of the modern corgi. This is an important link between the Egyptian house dog and the terriers which arose in Britain. When the Celts spread their wings even further and began to colonise Britain and Ireland, they would have brought their great hunting dogs with them. Hounds certainly came with them, for the old Irish hound (which is probably still to be found in quite a pure form in the shape of the Scottish deerhound) was from the stock used in Europe for hunting wolves etc. No doubt small dachshund/basset types and maybe rough-haired Maltese terrier types came too, as did the ancient corgi-like terrier. They probably also brought mastiffs and herding dogs with them. The Celts then, were the second key to the creation and development of our modern breeds.

The third key was the Romans, who took their favourite dogs with them on their numerous conquests. It is likely that they introduced dachshund- and mastiff-type dogs into places such as Germany, and greyhounds and mastiffs into Britain, along with other breeds. Finally, it was the turn of the Vikings, for they certainly brought with them herding dogs from more northern parts of Europe. These breeds gave rise to the border collie and others.

To summarise, the four keys to the creation and development of the strains that gave rise to our modern breeds, including terriers, were: the Phoenicians, who excelled at sea trading and played a major part in taking terrier and other types to Europe; the Celts, who took these and new breeds with them as they spread throughout Europe and eventually to Britain and Ireland; the Romans, who brought dachshund and greyhound types to Britain and northern parts of Europe, along with the mastiff of course; and the Vikings who were probably responsible for bringing most of the ancestors of our modern herding breeds to Britain.

When did terriers begin their long, relentless development to the breeds we know and love today? To answer this question we need to take a trip back in time to around 2,000 years ago. Small terrier/hound types were popular in Europe, and, as I have said, dachshund/basset types existed way back in Egypt and surrounding countries, as did Spanish terrier types. The Maltese and Spanish absorbed the small, rough-haired terrier types, and they gave rise to the Maltese and Greek breeds of long ago. The French were instrumental in creating small and large hounds from the breeds which arrived with the early sea traders. The Celts hunted and developed these still further, and later the Greeks and Romans hunted and bred them too. The Greek historian, Oppian, it seems, was himself involved in the breeding of small hound/terrier types which he considered well adapted to hunting in the woods. So we can conclude that from these basic breeds our terriers began to be developed. The very first terrier types though were brought to Britain by the Celts, however, records of their culture tell of small corgi/terrier types that came with them from Europe. From this type and the dachshund/basset and Maltese terrier breeds we get the foundation stock of our modern terrier breeds, though a very important ingredient had still to be added to the mixture.

Writing some 2,000 years ago, Gratius Falliscus tells of Roman molossus dogs (a larger type of mastiff) being pitted against British pugnaces (mastiffs) after the Roman invasion (proof that the Celts brought mastiffs at an earlier time), and he reports that the British pugnaces defeated their European cousins. This information is useful in that it is probably the earliest recorded dog fight in Britain, but what Falliscus goes on to tell us is far more interesting. He goes on to say that there were two different types of pugnaces in Britain; a large type which was capable of tackling both lions and bears (three were considered a fair match for a bear, while four were considered a fair match for a lion); and a small type which undoubtedly entered into the old terrier strains, giving courage and strength to the resultant offspring.

This smaller mastiff (sometimes called a degenerate mastiff), which was already breeding true to type as long ago as 2,000 years, is no doubt the ancestor of not only our modern terrier breeds, but also the bulldog, and possibly medium-sized hounds such as the beagle. From then on reports appear of terrier types which came mainly in two different varieties. Turbeville, writing in 1575, describes one variety as being short legged and the other rough coated and straight legged. Both types represent the odd mixture of dachshund/basset types, rough-haired Spanish and Greek terrier types, the little Celtic corgi type and the final ingredient which Falliscus told us about, the smaller type of mastiff. Later on, much more mastiff blood was added, as was beagle and small foxhound blood, crosses which produced much leggier terriers that became popular from the seventeenth century onwards, when fox hunting began to grow in popularity. The fact that terriers often hunt above ground lends weight to the theory that the hounds of old form part of their make-up. At Windmill hill in Wiltshire, evidence has been unearthed of ancient peoples (dating before 3000 BC) keeping fox-terrier-sized dogs which they used for hunting cats and foxes, but whether these were indeed terriers or small hounds is impossible to say. One thing is pretty certain, however: these types of dogs undoubtedly gave rise to the terriers of today.

Emerging from a deep rock pile.

From this rather mixed bunch of strains, our modern terrier breeds originated and have developed over many centuries into the types we now know and love. With a mixture such as this, is it any wonder that our modern terriers should come in such great variety, suited to so many different tasks?

2

The Traditional Role of Terriers

The Jack Russell Terrier

It was on a warm May afternoon in 1819 that Parson John Russell bought his first terrier from a milkman whom he met on the road to Marston. E.W.L. Davies, Russell's friend and biographer, possessed a copy of an oil painting of this famous terrier, Trump, and gives us a description so famous that I need not set it down here, for it is an oft-repeated quotation. However, for those who have never read his description of Trump, here it is:

> In the first place the colour is white with just a patch of dark tan over each eye and ear, while a similar dot, not larger than a penny piece, marks the root of the tail. The coat, which is thick, close and a trifle wiry, is well calculated to protect the body from wet and cold, but he's no affinity with the long, rough jacket of a Scotch terrier. The legs are straight as arrows, the feet perfect; the loins and conformation of the whole frame indicative of hardihood and endurance; while the size and height of the animal may be compared to that of a full-grown vixen fox.

Trump was most certainly a very 'typey' animal, and would win well at shows today. She has set the standard that not only Russell himself admired so much, but the one that is aimed for to this very day, for it is the official standard set for the Parson Jack Russell terrier, a breed now recognised by the Kennel Club – to the detriment of its working qualities in years to come I fear!

Parson Russell, though a great admirer of a good, 'typey' terrier, believed that gameness was the prime quality needed in an animal which was required to earn its keep at a southern hunt kennel. Trump was not only a beautiful-looking terrier, but also a game dog whom Russell would have tested to the full out in the hunting field, for he would surely not have used a non-worker, or even a poor worker, as the cornerstone of his strain of white-bodied terriers. Russell was a hunting man through and through and hunted foxes regularly for decades, so game terriers were essential.

Fox-hunting began to rise in popularity during the seventeenth and eighteenth centuries in particular; the fox was considered as vermin before its sporting potential began to be discovered by lovers of the chase, who had previously hunted the stag. Of course, foxes had been hunted with hounds long before then, but this kind of hunting was unpopular and carried out mainly by farmers or professional pest controllers, seeking foxes for the bounty that was offered. Most of these packs of hounds were trencher-fed and small in number and many of them died out rapidly when the gentry turned to fox-hunting instead.

Hound conformation improved drastically and great pride was taken in the appearance of the pack, and also the hunt servants too. Terriers at this time were rough-and-ready characters, used for sport, yes, but mainly for keeping down vermin such as rats, pole-cats, badgers, foxes and the occasional otter that had strayed from the river and had decided that the farmer's chickens or ducks would make a tasty change from fish and eels. These terriers suited farmers and pest controllers alike, but they did not suit the masters of the fine packs of foxhounds which began to be built up, for they undoubtedly spoiled the uniformity of the pack, not to mention the elegant hunters which were so precious to them.

There was only one thing to do, to breed terriers which would match their fine hounds, adding to the harmony which was so desired at the kennels and, more importantly, while out hunting. Small beagle blood was undoubtedly used to achieve this. Not only would it have resulted in better type and hound markings, but it would also have improved nose and voice in the resultant off-spring, essential qualities for the traditional working terrier.

Short legged and long backed, with prick-up ears; long haired, bent legged and bulky, with quite a long back; leggy, fairly short, with straight legs and a narrow front – these were three descriptions of the general type of terriers to be found during the seventeenth and eighteenth centuries, and these types were undoubtedly the basic ingredients which eventually gave rise to the terriers of today. Indeed, the Jack Russell comes in two distinct types; the short-legged, long-backed variety, usually under 12 in (30 cm), and the leggy variety, above 12 in, the type favoured by southern huntsmen before and during Russell's lifetime, and for very good reason.

The traditional role of this type of terrier, so beloved by John Russell, is clearly seen from one of his favourite stories concerning Tip, one of his best workers. At Brayford, in North Devon, Russell pointed out a favourite spot where he had found and flushed many foxes over the years, enjoying some cracking runs thereafter. He described the spot as 'a dark patch of hanging gorse . . . by yonder knoll' where he had seen 'many a good run from that sheltered nook'. Once again, they had found a fox at this same place which managed to beat them by reaching a big place known as Gray's Holt, the old Devonshire name for a badger sett, a notorious spot, huge and undiggable. Russell admitted that this was a formiddable place, even for the likes of 'Tip or the stoutest foe' as he put it.

They found this same fox lying up at this same spot again and Russell watched as Tip sped off across country at full speed. Jack Yelland, Russell's whipper-in at the time, shouted that he was off to Gray's Holt. He was right for, although the hounds were not pointing in that direction, Tip could be seen at the spot 'throwing his tongue frantically, doing his utmost by noise and gesture to scare away the fox from approaching the earths'. Tip succeeded for the fox 'passed onto the heather, and, after a clinking run, hounds killed Reynard on the moor'.

Clearly, Russell's terriers ran with hounds and would go to ground when they were needed, following by sight and sound and then by scent once the pack had forged on ahead. For a terrier to be capable of such feats, it would need to be 'up on the leg' because a short-legged, long-backed dog would find such a task impossible. They would also need a good nose in order to follow by scent, catching up with the pack at a difficult check or at an earth where their presence was eagerly awaited.

The hard, wiry jacket was preferred by Russell for obvious reasons. He hunted some bleak countryside, which is bitterly cold and often wet during the hunting season, and a terrier which was required to work regularly in such places would need maximum protection, especially at dusk when temperatures drop rapidly, for Russell would sometimes reach home long after darkness had set in. Although this hard, dense jacket was preferred by John Russell, it has to be said that the smooth-coated Russell has also worked in these same places and conditions, and copes with the bad weather well enough.

Foxes were, and still are, the principal quarry of the Jack Russell terrier, though it is no longer practical to run them with the pack. But they also make superb ratting, ferreting and mink-hunting terriers; their beagle ancestry providing a wonderful nose that stands them in good stead for such tasks.

Jack Russells were never required to attack their fox, killing it underground or maybe damaging it before it bolted to hounds, making a good run impossible. Russell and other southern huntsmen, required their terriers to stand off their fox and bay at it, bolting it or guiding the diggers if it refused to bolt; and they require the same today. The addition of bull terrier blood often ruined these qualities and made a terrier rush in and attack its fox, eventually killing it and taking much punishment in the process. This was a type that was decried by the Parson. Today it is the addition of fell terrier blood that is making the Jack Russell too hard, although it is improving type dramatically, giving leg, a hard coat and a straight, narrow front to the old strains.

The old Jack Russell strains, or fox terriers as they were then known, certainly entered the old fell strains and some of these fell-bred Russells are throwbacks to the terrier type favoured by Russell and other terriermen such as Arthur Heinemann – better types, in fact, than many of the so-called 'pure' strains of Jack Russell still around today.

In fact, the terriers I have seen which are nearest to the standard set by Trump, have mainly been from fell-bred Russell types, although the 'stand back and bay' qualities have sadly often been lost. Billy, a fell-bred Russell bred by Gary Middleton, was a superb-looking terrier of the type nearest to Trump and this terrier, a hard worker whom Gary retired early after he had lost many of his teeth, has given rise to most of the fell-bred Jack Russells that are clearing up at the shows today. Billy is from Gary's old strain, which goes back to the two white terriers reputedly descended from Heinemann's strain of Jack Russell. These two Russell types were possibly descended from Linton Jack, a terrier descended from Russell's terriers, so these white fell-bred Russells may be able to claim descent from the original strain of Parson Russell himself!

The Border Terrier

Described as 'as game as they come' the border terrier is a very attractive, workmanlike animal that has been used in the hunting field for the past 200 years or so, though the early strain undoubtedly sprang from the mismatch of hardy working terriers which have been used in the north for centuries.

The border terrier of the latter part of the nineteenth century had quite a narrow head with a fairly poor, snipey jaw, but the muzzle was not as 'squat' as it is today – though the jaw is now more powerful than it was back then. Otter, marten, fox and badger were all considered fair game for this breed, which was considered fearless, and the border certainly excelled at otter hunting in particular, a love of water being just one of its many attributes. Like the Jack Russell, the border terrier ran with hounds in the days when it was possible to hunt in such a way, and this breed is superbly adapted to a vigorous hunting life in the north of England, where the country is rugged and windswept, plagued by thick, heavy mist and driving rain. It is up on the leg – essential for running with a pack of hounds – and has a hard, wiry and dense jacket, usually red grizzle or wheaten in colour. Many are a little too large in the chest for my liking, though there are plenty that are still narrow enough to 'get'. A roomy chest is essential in a working terrier, but a big barrel chest is not desirable, for this would hamper a terrier's progress underground. I have seen a border terrier 14 in (35 cm) tall and narrow at the shoulders, yet with enough chest room for strong heart and lungs, squeeze through a gap in the rocks where my larger fell terriers failed to 'get'.

Many view the border as a dog which will stand off its fox and bay, guiding the diggers in the same manner as a traditional Jack Russell, but this simply is not a true picture of this breed. Many border terriers, after becoming experienced at their work, will often take to killing their foxes if they refuse to bolt, although it has to be said that most are sensible enough to stay out of trouble and avoid serious injury through severe fox bites.

This ability to stay out of trouble is valued highly among experienced terriermen, for they know that a terrier which constantly gets himself badly knocked about will work one day and then be laid up for three or four weeks afterwards while his wounds heal, leading to a very limited working period during the season and usually a short career. The terrier who stands back and bays, or kills its fox cleverly and quickly, usually by throttling it as a lion kills its prey, will give its owner consistent work throughout the season for upwards of ten or eleven years, thus earning its keep twice over. I once used a border terrier to ground in a huge rockpile and, though he remained at his fox for over twenty-four hours, he avoided serious injury and was ready to go again a couple of days later. Terriers of this sort are worth their weight in gold.

I have a soft spot for a good working border terrier, though many are a little too shy for my liking. It is also true that many borders have little idea of what work is about, sometimes even as late as two years of age, a hereditary fault in some strains. Despite this, however, they come highly recommended as a working dog and, once entered, will make superb fox-bolting and digging terriers. A good border terrier will soon become an expert at bolting reluctant foxes, a rare quality that should make them more popular as a hunt terrier!

As I have said, they have a superb weatherproof coat that is easily cleaned and takes little effort to maintain. Simply plucking out the dead hair will keep it close, neat and tidy, though you should never cut or shave the jacket, as this will ruin it, making it soft and less able to cope with bad weather conditions. The coat of the border terrier is so valuable that I know of more than one top fell-terrier breeder who has brought this breed into their strains to improve coat type, and to give them sense when working below ground. Better, stronger heads usually result from this cross too. Always buy or use a border stud from a good, reliable working strain. This will ensure that you get terriers of the right sort – workers.

The coat of the border terrier also provides excellent protection when working thick cover for rabbits, mink and, their more traditional quarry, foxes.

An example of a good head on a border terrier, a fine quality that is used on many fell strains.

The Fell Terrier

Cumbria is a rugged, mountainous region, harsh – some would say hostile – with craggy peaks that reach up, one after another, into an often stormy sky, black and forbidding. When it rains, it *rains*, as anyone who has been unfortunate enough to be caught out in one of Cumbria's sudden, savage storms will testify. I was out with my family in the Lake District when one of these sudden storms struck. The heavens opened and we all ran for the car and shelter. But it was pointless for, within a few seconds, we were all soaked to the skin.

D.B. Plummer's *The Fell Terrier* had just been published and I had gone to the Lakes with a very different view of the region. Until that time, I had been a Jack Russell enthusiast, but from then on I developed a passion for the fell terrier, a passion which remains with me.

Cumbria is a hard place for those who attempt to make a living from its high, rocky slopes, keeping sheep – mainly the hardy herdwick – and a few chickens, ducks or geese around the farmyard. The tough fell foxes can take a heavy toll on a farmer's livestock. Many

Fell terriers in typical fell hunting country; a hard landscape for terriers to work successfully.

24

live in the shelter of the woodlands of the lower dales where food is easily obtained, but a surprising number of them also inhabit the mountainous regions, living among the often inaccessible crags and the deep, dark borrans, or rockpiles, and finding food as best they can, often by visiting the lower vales, or maybe one of the lonely farmsteads where fat hens are often found. It was to control these predators that the fell terrier was produced. Unlike the Jack Russell and the border terrier, which were created and used mainly for sport, the fell terrier was to be used as a protector of the hill shepherd's flocks, as a guardian of the farmyard, a much tougher role to fulfil.

Upon rising a farmer will often discover some of his livestock missing, or lying dead, attacked by a fox, which had returned to his lair, high up the fellside, on the narrow ledge of a crag or deep inside a rockpile. The farmer will get in touch with the huntsman of his local pack of fell hounds, which will be brought to the scene of the crime and take up the scent, following its line up the fellside until they eventually reach its lair, flushing it from the crag or marking it to ground. This is when the tough northern huntsmen will turn to their even tougher little terriers. The farmer will always want this kind of fox dealt with, and so a hard fell terrier will be entered in the hope that he will kill his fox below ground. Sometimes the fox will bolt and then hounds will hunt him.

It is not about sport, although hunting on the fells provides plenty of sport for those who appreciate hound work of the best sort. It is about control and the fell terrier plays a vital role in the economy of the English Lake District alongside the fellhounds and hunt servants.

Fell terriers often ran with hounds in the past, but this is now impossible due to the strict badger laws and increasing road traffic. They were traditionally up on the leg and big enough in the chest to cope with such a life, although they would still need to be narrow enough to creep through the rocks when working an earth.

Not all fell terriers are hard; many, if not most, will stand off their fox and bay, though some will wait their chance and then move in for the kill, throttling the fox. Some fell terriers do become hard to the point where they take punishment and serious injury, but most are clever enough to stay out of trouble, often getting this sense from border terrier blood which has been used in the strain at some point. Terriers that rush into an earth and are injured are not of the traditional type. A fell terrier must earn its keep working the big fell earths three or four days a week, from early September until as late as the middle of May, for as many as ten or eleven seasons in some cases, so those that get themselves badly damaged, needing weeks at a time to recover, are nigh on useless to a pack.

The image of the crazed dog keen to latch onto anything in its path, could not be further from the truth. The real fell terrier is quiet and docile and is often kennelled with hounds, though they make good house dogs too, for they love a warm fireside and do best in the company of other dogs.

A fell terrier checking out a borran (a naturally formed rock pile). Foxes love these types of earth.

Looking for foxes among a man-made rock pile.

3

Choosing and Caring for a Puppy

Before rushing out and buying the first puppy you see advertised, it is wise to sit down and have a good think about the breed of terrier which is best suited to your needs. What type of country will your dog be hunting? What exactly is it that you require of it? What will be its quarry and does size matter? These are the main things to consider before purchasing a puppy.

The main breeds which give a good account of themselves in the field are border, fell, Jack Russell, Bedlington, Plummer and Lucas terriers, although the latter are not yet as readily available as the others. But you may also be interested in one of the many pedigree breeds which, in the main, are no longer used for sporting purposes.

My advice is always to buy only from stock which are proven workers in all aspects of hunting. That means dogs that will readily find, bolt or stay to foxes below ground. Of course, it is also important that they should be keen while hunting rats and rabbits, or possibly mink, and maybe you are happy enough to buy a puppy from stock which spend their time hunting such quarry. However, I love to see an all-round terrier at its work, busily hunting rats, rabbits, mink and foxes, as competent above ground as below. Even when the owner is not seeking to catch a fox, a good terrier will often come across one, either lying up in thick undergrowth, or skulking in the darkness below ground. You may be surprised how eagerly your terrier takes to hunting foxes, even though they may not be on your quarry list; centuries of breeding for fox control come to the fore and drive the dog eagerly on with a natural instinct.

If you are serious about working one of the pedigree breeds, then look for a breeder who still works his stock regularly, testing them to the full out in the open field rather than in the showring, so that you know what to expect. And always find out how the parents cope in bad weather conditions and ask to see them so that you can check for yourself that the coat is of a sort that gives sufficient

Fell terrier with a good, hard jacket, the type that gives maximum protection against bad weather.

protection from the elements – an essential requirement which becomes more important as the climate changes.

A good coat type is second in importance only to the need to buy a puppy from the right stock – good workers. A terrier's coat has always been a priority, especially for those who hunt hilly and mountainous country, and hard, wiry jackets have been, for centuries, the most desirable type, – and no wonder, for the high ground is plagued with the severest of weather conditions. It is a tough enough life under the best of conditions, but can be lethal to a terrier with a poor, open coat which spends hour after hour crossing a bleak fell top, through freezing becks and over snow-covered or wet terrain, and is then being required to go to ground, tackle a tough hill fox in a frozen drain or a damp, draughty rockpile and then, after all this, take the long trek home. Only the fittest and best-equipped terriers could hope to cope well with such an existence.

Open moorlands and exposed fell tops are bitterly cold places during the autumn, winter and early spring; they are rarely what you would call warm even during the height of summer, when a chill breeze usually blows. With the weather patterns changing, becoming much wetter than we are already used to in this country, the winds stronger and extremely cold, the importance of a good jacket in an exposed landscape becomes even more essential. In wet and windy conditions, especially when a freezing wind blows, a terrier can chill badly, especially when the coat is loose and open, lacking a thick undercoat and density.

The best jacket for these conditions is undoubtedly a close, iron-hard coat which sheds water quickly and keeps out much of the wind, though if it is dense, with a good undercoat, it will give much protection in most conditions. Even if the jacket is smooth, known as 'slape-coated' amongst fell-terrier breeders, it will give plenty of protection as long as it has enough density. Brian Nuttall and John Parks are best known for breeding these slape-coated terriers and this type has been tested from Land's End to John O'Groats and not been found wanting. Brian Nuttall loans his terriers out to various hunts and he once told me that he had two at the Eskdale and Ennerdale Hunt which covers some of the wettest and windiest places in England, so these jackets must give enough protection to the terriers who are required to work successfully in such places. In fact, Cyril Breay, the founder, together with the legendary Frank Buck, of these slape-coated black, black and tan, red and sometimes chocolate fell terriers, often called Patterdales, hunted his dogs with the Lunesdale Foxhounds where some of the bleakest and most exposed of fells and moors make up much of the hunt's country, and they obviously coped well enough in all weathers. When he was interviewed by Brian Plummer for his masterpiece, *The Fell Terrier*, Maurice Bell, master and huntsman of the Wensleydale Foxhounds, mentioned that Cyril Breay's terriers were often uncomfortable or unhappy, when standing around in severe weather, but I think this is true no matter what the coat type. I have yet to see a terrier that was not uncomfortable standing around in a freezing gale. No matter how wrapped up you may be, if you stand still for long enough in bad weather, you will soon begin to feel unhappy. However, I do agree with Maurice's preference for a close, iron-hard jacket on a terrier, for this gives maximum protection and the terrier with this type of coat does indeed suffer less.

A silky-soft coat which lacks density is to be avoided, no matter how well the parents work, for this jacket gives little resistance to bad weather and a terrier will suffer badly on chilly days. It may even suffer shock and die when the weather is at its worst. I had a terrier which developed this type of coat. I was entering her for a friend who let me have her on loan for a couple of seasons. She came

A slape-coated terrier. This dense type of jacket gives plenty of protection from the elements.

to me stripped out and it was not until later, when her fur began to grow back, that I realised she had a terrible coat, not at all suitable for the hilly districts that I hunt, so she was quickly returned and ended up as a pet.

Brian Plummer, in *The Fell Terrier*, mentions a terrier owned by Braithwaite Wilson by the name of Betty. This bitch entered a rock earth and accounted for its fox below ground in good fell-terrier fashion, becoming trapped for three days in blizzard conditions. The Ullswater Foxhounds, whose huntsman Wilson was at the time, hunt some of the coldest and wildest spots in Britain, open and exposed to the severest of weather conditions, and this bitch undoubtedly survived her ordeal because she was of the type Wilson favoured, extremely hard coated. Many terriers descended from dogs which were bred and worked in the Ullswater country, produce this iron-hard, dense jacket to this day, Betty's line being continued through the terriers of Sid and Joe Wilkinson and later, Gary Middleton. Some of the best weatherproof jackets today are to be found on Gary's terriers.

Parson Russell himself, a man who hunted a lot of exposed moor-land in the south of England, favoured a hard, wiry jacket on his

The Lakes country; terriers need a good dense jacket in such a landscape.

fox terriers, though this type of coat has become increasingly difficult to find on Jack Russells in recent decades. Many Russell
enthusiasts are turning to the white lakeland terrier, particularly
Gary Middleton's famous stud dog, Billy, or his sons and grandsons
in order to put the wire and density back into these strains. The
Parson Jack Russell terrier which is now recognised by the Kennel
Club, to the detriment of its working qualities I fear (as few show
dogs are actually used for work), is particularly affected though the
unregistered strains too, are saturated with the blood of white lakelands as breeders obsessively strive to produce a perfect 14 in
(35 cm) 14 lb (6 kg) terrier of the type closest to the standard set by
Trump. Likewise, fell or lakeland terrier breeders are putting pedigree lakeland and fox terrier blood back into the old strains in search
of the perfect box-shaped lakeland and are ruining the working
qualities so desired in a terrier by the old fell huntsmen. They
produce fiery fighting dogs with little, if any, sense underground
and very often a lack of hunting instinct. Avoid like the plague

Tarn and Beck, a Russell type with lakeland blood.

any fell terriers which display pedigree lakeland blood in their make-up. It was possible to use this cross and still produce workers, a little more fiery perhaps, in decades gone by, but I would not advise it today, when very few terriers of the pedigree variety are worked.

Having decided upon a puppy from proven working stock and having settled upon the best coat type for the country you will be hunting, it is now time to choose the breed. Jack Russells, which are free of lakeland terrier blood, those of the old traditional type bred and worked by such men as Eddie Chapman, Arthur Nixon and David Jones, make superb all-rounders, above and below ground, hunting a line extremely keenly and throwing tongue in a way that betrays their beagle ancestry and, when up to a fox inside an earth, standing off their quarry and baying for all they are worth. This ability to stand off and bay at a fox, thus bolting it undamaged to the waiting pack, or noisily guiding diggers to the spot, was highly prized by such notables as John Russell, Arthur Heinemann and, later, Dan Russell, for they valued a terrier that respected its quarry, did not damage it in any way, and came away from the encounter unharmed. In fact, the stand-off and bay quali-ties of Russells made them very popular with badger-digging clubs and otter hunters, for hard terriers suffered badly when

A litter of Jack Russell pups bred by myself.

encountering a brock or a striking otter and, as a result, could not be regularly worked to such quarry owing to the injuries received.

If you need a good, all-round terrier that has good nose, voice and sense enough to stay out of trouble, then Jack Russells, without either lakeland or bull terrier blood (most terriers have bull terrier blood in their distant ancestry), may well suit your needs.

However, if you hunt a country with huge rockpiles, old mineshafts and other undiggable earths, then in my view the traditional Jack Russell terrier is of limited use. In places such as the Lake District, the mountainous regions of Wales, the high country of Scotland, the fells of north Yorkshire and the hilly parts of Lancashire and Derbyshire, many of the earths are big and often undiggable, and foxes can find themselves a good vantage point from which they are extremely reluctant to move, especially when confronted with a yappy Jack Russell which is not able to push a stubborn fox hard in order to persuade it that making a bid for open country is by far the best option. A fell terrier, or an experienced border terrier, will usually shift foxes from such an earth, if they are bred right, for the fell terrier specialises in tackling its fox hard but cleverly, bolting or killing it without taking severe punishment. They have been bred this way out of necessity, for fell foxes must be controlled in what is principally sheep-rearing country. As I have said, border terriers, with experience, soon develop the knack of shifting reluctant foxes and this quality was bred into the old fell strains.

A huge borran high up in the western Pennines, a wild, windswept country.

Where foxes are hunted in order to protect livestock, those that will not shift will be dealt with underground. Again, the fell terrier which bays at its fox until it is able to get a grip and throttle it is desirable for this type of work, and undoubtedly the best kind are those which have border blood in their bloodlines, giving them sense, but keeping the courage of the traditional fell terriers hunted by such legends as Joe Bowman and Willie Porter.

If you will be hunting this type of country, then fell or border terriers come highly recommended (I include white lakelands when I talk about fell terriers), though many borders are now being bred with large chests and small, squat heads, some even with poor coats – too soft and silky – and these are best avoided by the serious fox hunter. Always buy a border terrier from working stock, for far too many strains are no longer worked these days and their original qualities, once cherished by fox and otter hunters, have suffered greatly.

A fell terrier with much border blood in its make-up.

Does size matter when it comes to working terriers? When I interviewed Wendy Pinkney, daughter of Maurice Bell and wife of Will, the Pennine Foxhounds huntsman, she summed the matter up far better than I could hope to do. She does not really mind what the size of a working terrier is, as long as it is spannable* and narrow enough in the chest to squeeze through tight spaces. Bedlington terriers, quite a large breed, have enjoyed a great revival, ever since George Newcombe of north Yorkshire produced smaller, more capable Bedlingtons by introducing fell terrier blood into the lines of pedigree Bedlingtons and, by breeding away from this cross, has put the hunting and working instinct back into this north-eastern

* If your thumbs and fingers meet when placed around the chest, just behind the front legs, then a terrier is said to be 'spannable', indicating that it can negotiate tight places below ground.

breed, which was once much favoured as a sporting beast. As a result of this, Bedlingtons now have a large following amongst those who love an all-rounder. Though they are in the main, a little larger than the other breeds mentioned, many are able to get to ground simply because they are narrow enough in the chest and are spannable, folding their long legs in order to get through tight spaces as they follow the fox underground.

Wendy once told me about a small terrier she had bred and how it struggled to follow across rough ground, especially through deep heather up on the high moorland which makes up a good deal of the Pennine Foxhounds country, and she stressed quite strongly the need for a terrier to be up on the leg in such a country. Although many of her terriers reach 12 or 13 in (30–33 cm) at the shoulder, they all have sufficient leg length to cope with rough country, while a short-legged terrier would find it almost impossible in these conditions. I have to agree, for I hunt some rough places – scattered rock and scree, heather over a foot deep in places – and a leggy terrier will negotiate such a landscape without too many problems. The short-legged variety would be exhausted just trying to keep up, and would probably not have enough energy left when asked to do its job.

Terriers with a bit of leg length are the best type for working this type of earth.

A fell terrier on a Lakeland mountain. In the old days, fell terriers often followed hounds and needed to be leggy to do so.

I like a bit of leg length on a terrier required to work rockpiles and crags, as this enables them to jump on and off rock ledges and to nego-tiate the often slippery sides of the huge boulders which are often encountered at these earths. For the terrier who hunts lowland pastures and gentle rolling hills with woodland included, encoun-tering stone drains and dug-out rabbit warrens, length of leg begins to fade in importance, but for the one hunting rough ground, old quar-ries, mineshafts and rockpiles, leg length is essential. While on holiday in the Lake District, I was browsing through a bookshop and came across a book containing old photographs of Cumbrian life. There was a picture of the Eskdale and Ennerdale Foxhounds with Willie Porter and a few terriers standing amongst a huge Lakeland borran. Some of these terriers were old fashioned Russell types (though they may have been fell-bred) and though they were only around 12 in (30 cm) tall, they had enough length of leg to be able to cope with the hard country hunted by this well-known pack. So leggy terriers have always found favour in these northern districts and 13 or 14 in (33–35 cm) terriers are undoubtedly the most useful. I have an engraving of Ambleside in the 1830s and it shows a huntsman leading his pack out of the village and with him are a couple of undocked, dark-coloured terriers with narrow shoulders and plenty of leg.

Even bigger terriers of around 15 or 16 in (38–40 cm) at the shoulder should not be ruled out, as long as they are narrow chested and spannable. Ghyll, a Parks-bred, slape-coated terrier, was a big, powerful dog of around 15 in (38 cm) and he usually got to his fox in the end, even though he had to dig on in some of the tighter places on occasion. There is more of a risk of a larger terrier becoming trapped below ground however, owing to the build-up of soil and loose stone that the terrier has put behind it whilst digging on. I should not worry too much, however, for the risk is minimal. I once watched one of my fell terriers, Turk, a Middleton-bred dog a little larger than Ghyll and extremely strong willed, squeeze through a very narrow rock crevice which was full of fox scent and make his way out the other side. He was just about spannable too. And do not forget, foxes are far more slender and agile than even small terriers, so there will always be places where a dog cannot follow, no matter how game it is. On several occasions over the years I have had to leave foxes, in rock especially, that have climbed up an impossibly narrow crevice where the terriers simply cannot get, despite their best efforts. Only recently I was out with Mist and Fell, my two fell terriers, at an old quarry and I saw Mist taking more than a casual interest in a thick covert. Fell joined her and both

Bella (right) with her dam Rock. She was sired by Chris Rainford's Snap, a top class working dog. Always breed or buy from workers.

made their way into the covert and fell silent. I made my way through the thick tangle of undergrowth and soon came across a rock earth where I could hear them marking, keen to a frenzy almost, obviously unable to reach their fox. They tried everything to get to it, probably one of that year's cubs just starting out on its own and able to get into some incredibly narrow places. In the end, after a great deal of effort, we gave it best and will no doubt hunt it another day.

When you have sought out the correct coat type and size for the country you hunt, it all comes down to one thing in the end: heart. The most important thing in the make-up of any working terrier, no matter what the breed or type, is how game it is. If a terrier has gameness – enough heart to do its job well even under the worst of conditions – then you cannot go far wrong and by purchasing a puppy from working stock, you are doing your utmost to ensure that you are getting the ingredients which will produce a good worker in the future.

Of course, you could buy a terrier which is already entered, saving you lots of time and energy, but there are real dangers in doing so. *Always* find out the reason for the sale. Many terrier sales really are for genuine reasons, often because the owner is over-stocked, and some excellent workers can be obtained (at a price) in this way. However, the terrier may be for sale because it lacks interest in its work, has become a quitter (usually because of wrong training and entering practices, though not always, for some just do not have the heart for their work) or has become too hard and stupid (sometimes due to premature entering). It is these that you should avoid, no matter how tempted you are. The best way to avoid ending up with an almost useless animal is to ask for a trial so that you can see for yourself how it works and how it responds to commands etc., always making sure that it has been properly broken to livestock. In this way you can ensure that you do not get lumbered with a terrier that is far more of a liability than an asset.

I have acquired some excellent working terriers, even without a trial, but only when I have known and trusted the person I have been doing business with. But generally if you cannot get a trial, then my advice is, unless you know and trust the seller, then do not buy, for you are asking for trouble. It is far better to go out and buy a puppy and bring it on yourself.

Having decided what you are looking for, you need to consult those publications most likely to contain the right advertisements, the *Countryman's Weekly*, *Loot* and *Exchange & Mart*. When you find a litter and go and inspect it, the best advice I can give is to pick the puppy that catches your eye the most, and only buy a pup from a healthy litter that has clearly been looked after well. Cold noses, clean and shiny eyes and coats and a certain playfulness are good indicators that a litter has been cared for properly. If the kennel is filthy, the pups lifeless and shivery, their coats dirty, their skin breaking out in little rashes, the eyes lacking interest, then do not buy, just get out of there as soon as possible. It is a matter of common sense really, and picking the one which most appeals to you is the best policy.

Despite what many books say, I would not rule out buying the puppy which is the timid one of the litter, I can remember picking up my puppy from a litter a friend of mine had bred. I had a choice of two bitches and went for the boldest of the pair, the other was shy and stayed away from me while 'mine' was friendly and playful. My wife wanted the shy pup, but I, following all the advice I had read, picked the more outgoing bitch. In the end she grew to be a slow starter and an inconsistent worker until she matured well into her second season, while the shy pup, the one I had rejected, grew into a cracking worker at an early age and was flying to ground from the beginning of her career. So do not rule out the shy puppy in the litter. If it catches your eye and you fancy it, then why not?

There is nothing wrong in asking to see the parents. Very often the sire belongs to someone else, so this is not always possible, but there may be a photograph you can look at. You may even be bold enough to ask if you can have a day out in order to see how they work before you buy, although I think the breeder would be most unlikely to agree and anyway, if you buy from a reputable breeder who is well known for producing good workers, then it is unnecessary to see the parents at work. Terriermen who have built up good reputations in this way will not sell stock from non-workers, so you cannot go far wrong when you buy from reliable sources.

If the puppies have been allowed to play with toys or there is enough bedding for you to take part of it away with you, then feel free to ask for something which carries the scent of the other litter members and, more importantly, the dam, as this will help the puppy to settle down during the night and at other times when it will be left alone. Even if you have bought two puppies, whether from the same litter or different ones, or you already have another dog at home, then the new puppy will usually still cry at night and when left alone, and some item with the scent of its family on it will often help to comfort it at these times. A ticking clock, or a radio playing quietly may also help to settle a young pup when it finds itself in unfamiliar surroundings. Many books claim that a ticking clock sounds similar to the dam's heartbeat to a lonely puppy, but I do not agree with this theory. I just think that the constant ticking has a calming effect and helps the pup to relax and fall asleep.

It is essential to keep your new puppy in dry, comfortable surroundings if it is going to thrive and grow. Some prefer to kennel a dog outside, while others would much rather have it in the house as part of the family. From my own experience of both kennelling terriers and housing them with the family, I believe that keeping a terrier in the home is by far the best option. Of course, an outside kennel may be the only option open to you, especially if you are going to be keeping large numbers of dogs in the future. I enjoy the company of a brace of working terriers around the house, but always keep any others outside in a kennel and run.

It is impossible to keep a puppy in a totally draught-free environment, but it is important to make sure that the kennel and run are well maintained and dry. Good maintenance will also prevent your terrier from scratching or chewing its way out and escaping. A kennel of around 6 ft x 3 ft (2 m x 1 m) is a decent size for no more than a brace of terriers, with a run of 6 ft x 6 ft (2 m x 2 m) attached to it. The sleeping compartment should be roomy enough for two and well padded with newspaper and an old blanket, raised off the floor to help keep the cold out and always with the entrance turned away from the door and the hole which leads into the run, in order to help shelter the puppy from any draughts that could seriously threaten its health if left unchecked.

I believe it is always much better to have two dogs together than one on its own, though never three, for serious fights can sometimes break out and two will gang up on one and may cause very serious injury, or even kill it. Make sure, moreover, that the two being kept together get on, even if they sleep separately as mine do. This is especially true if the dog is kennelled and spends a lot of time away from the family, though I would recommend a companion for a house dog too.

Terriers which are kept in the house and spend a lot of time with children and other family members, possibly growing up with a cat around the place, make stock-breaking easy and will usually be easier to train as they are far more socialised than those kept outside. Terriers kept outside will have far less contact with cats, visitors to the home, other dogs etc. And it is much easier to train a puppy which is around you for much of the day, for your training sessions can be more frequent than if it is kept outside, especially during the cold

Mist and Turk enjoying home comforts.

winter months when you will not want to spend much time outside.

There are many excellent puppy foods on the market. You may ask the breeder what he has been feeding the litter so that you can carry on with this feeding programme, and so avoid the upset stomach that always seems to accompany a change of feed, or you may settle upon a certain brand which you prefer; it is up to you. A puppy usually gets a bit of an upset stomach anyway, from the trauma of leaving its family and being put into an alien environment. The breeder may provide you with a few days' worth of feed so that you can mix it with the puppy's new food, cutting down on the old stuff each day, and thus slowly changing its diet. I use this method and it works very well indeed.

When you reach home, it is a good idea to give your puppy a light meal and offer it some fresh water with the chill taken out of it with hot water from the kettle (but always check the temperature before offering it to the puppy), or maybe some warm milk watered down a little to avoid upsetting its stomach. I always provide a saucer of warm watered-down milk with every meal. Remember always to provide fresh water, whether outside or inside, though not in a deep dish – there is always the danger of a puppy falling into a deep dish, or even a mop bucket with water left in it, and drowning, so make sure that its environment is safe, as you would with a child. Also be aware of wires that may be exposed and be chewed by the youngster, with fatal consequences. Feeding a newly arrived pup will help it to settle and go to sleep. Spend as much time as possible on this first day, and subsequent days, weeks and months of course, playing with it and getting it used to your scent, scent that can be rubbed on its bedding, helping it to settle at night, or during the day while you are out.

Some books will tell you to feed a puppy four or even five times per day and, while this may be good advice for the bigger breeds, I have found it unnecessary for terrier pups who thrive very well on just three meals per day. Quantity is difficult to be precise about as no two pups have exactly the same requirements, so the best advice I can offer is to feed your puppy until it turns away from its dish with a huge, swollen belly that gives it a comical appearance as it wobbles across the floor, unable to eat any more. After all, when suckling, they take milk until they are full, and so until they reach twelve weeks of age, they can continue to do so. You will soon get to know, as your puppy grows and you get used to feeding it, how much to give. It is a simple matter of observing your pup. It should always carry some fat, so if it begins to look a little on the skinny side, then increase the quantity of feed; if it becomes too obese, then decrease the quantity. Again, it is a matter of common sense and experience is usually the best teacher in these matters.

I give cereal for the first meal of the day (Weetabix is very good for puppies), with a little watered down warm milk, puppy meat and biscuits at dinner time (you will have to give this meal at tea time if you are out at work all day) and again at around 6.30 (bed time if you are at work all day). I make sure that there is plenty of food for this last meal so that the puppy can return to it a little later, helping it to settle for the night. I keep this feeding programme going until the pup is four months old, at which stage I cut out the dinner-time meal. When it reaches eight months, I cut out its breakfast, and it will have just one meal a day from then on.

Puppies which are wormed regularly do best and there are some good remedies on the market today. I find the chocolate-flavoured liquid to be very effective and usually give it every fortnight until the puppy reaches twelve weeks, when I do it every three months until it reaches twelve months of age; a single tablet every six months is best from then on. These tablets are available at your local vet and are multi-wormers. Keeping your terrier flea-free is essential if it is to be rid of worms. Again, the vet can provide you with the best products for killing fleas, which are an absolute nuisance, especially during a hot summer when they will reach plague proportions if you are not careful.

When your puppy reaches twelve weeks of age, it is time to take it to the vet for the first of its inoculations, the second being given a couple of weeks later, and these are absolutely essential. Remember never to allow your youngster to go beyond your own garden, and to ensure that street curs cannot wander into it, until it has received both inoculations, as you could easily end up with a very sick puppy that has picked up distemper or some other potentially fatal disease. If your garden is fenced off so that no other dogs can use it, then your puppy should be safe enough. If it is not, then it is best to confine the puppy to its kennel and run or to the house.

Pups should be kept clean and warm and should be wormed regularly.

4

Training and Stock-breaking

Terriers are extremely strong-willed little creatures and the 'firm but fair' method is best when starting their training programme. Training a young terrier can often be a battle of wills, but if the dog gets boss of its owner it will soon grow into a nuisance and a liability as it becomes more and more uncontrollable until the only options left are either to part with it to someone who can try to cure it of its bad habits or to have it put down, often the kindest thing to do as some terriers cannot be broken of bad habits especially sheep worrying, no matter how hard one tries. So be firm when training your puppy and do not allow it to get its own way or look the other way when it is up to mischief. Instead, make sure that you always act quickly to check any signs of bad behaviour. When you give a command, make sure that the dog carries it out; do not allow it to ignore you.

Getting the puppy to come to you is both essential and simple enough. Call it to you with an encouraging, enthusiastic voice; it may also help to bend down or even sink to your knees, maybe even putting your head down to the ground, all acts that will arouse curiosity in a youngster and will usually get its attention. When it obeys and comes to you, reward it with plenty of excited praise, stroking and patting it and playing little games with it. You may even decide to reward it with some suitable dog chocolates, or with little puppy biscuits; I find that these work well enough, especially when the youngster is a little reluctant to come to you. Getting a puppy coming to you when called is the first stage of its training programme and can be started as soon as you get it home. Just playing with it while frequently using its name, calling it to you and enthusiastically praising it and rewarding it will help to convince a pup that the best policy is to go to its master when called, especially when the experience is pleasant and rewarding, attractive to a curious youngster.

All puppies are different. Some will run away from you when you call them, while others, almost from day one, will come readily when called. Turk, a fell terrier dog from the Middleton bloodlines, was a swine for running away in the opposite direction whenever I called him in, and he would do his utmost to avoid me, spending an age rooting around the garden, hunting squirrels and chasing young birds around the trees while ignoring my calls from the back door. He was hyperactive and developed behavioural problems too, but I soon had him coming in when called after he had discovered that chocolates were his reward for doing so. Mist, on the other hand, a good-looking bitch who is a mixture of Ward, Middleton, Cowan, Gould and Frank Buck bloodlines, has almost from the beginning proved extremely obedient and was a delight to train. Stock-breaking was easy with her and it is a delight to work her, for I know I can trust her, as she responds to commands very quickly indeed. She sometimes needs a few harsh words, but that is usually all it takes. Although some terriers may need a firmer hand, they should never be beaten.

Mist does have her faults however. She is shy with strangers and this can be a nuisance at times. I was once high up on a fell top deep in the heart of Borrowdale, searching for the Blencathra Foxhounds after they had disappeared into woodland below, hot on the fox's tail. An elderly gentleman approached to ask if I had seen the hounds and he soon began to tell me some fascinating tales of his days following this famous pack. I could have spent an age listening to him, but Mist kept growling and barking at him.

While the first stage of training proceeds from the very first day, housetraining if your puppy will be living indoors should also begin from the very moment you arrive home for, at eight weeks – the usual age at which puppies are allowed to be parted from their family – it will urinate and defecate rather frequently and you must never turn a blind eye and allow it to get away with messing indoors. It must quickly learn to associate messing in the house with punishment and unpleasantness, and that means you must be observant, learning to recognise the signs that your pup needs to go out. Be persistent in this regard. When your pup urinates or defecates, show it the offending mess immediately (never rub its nose in it, this is both cruel and unnecessary), tap it gently on the nose with your finger and say firmly, though not harshly, 'No', repeating this a few times. Then carry it out to the garden, saying 'Outside' as you go and put it down on the grass (use a litter tray by the back door until it is inoculated if your garden is not fenced off to street curs). Do this consistently until the youngster begins to get the idea and goes to the door of its own accord. So be observant and, when your pup has gone to the door and then gone outside, make a real fuss of it and reward it generously. Some learn this lesson quickly, while others can take several weeks to catch on. My fell terrier bitch, Rock, began asking to go outside after only three days of training, while Ghyll took an age to catch on. Mist got the idea very quickly indeed, after only a few days, but then relapsed for a while before beginning to ask to go out once more.

Confining a puppy to a small space, no less than 6 ft x 3 ft (2 m x 1 m), with old newspaper left on the floor is best during the night, when it will be unable to hold itself until morning, but it is vital that you show it the mess in the morning and repeat the procedure used during the daytime, taking it outside as normal. It could be a few months before a youngster is completely clean at night, but again, it may learn very quickly indeed.

If your terrier is persistently dirty during the night and looks as though it will never learn to be clean, then confining it inside a terrier box during the night with enough room for it to be comfortable but no more, may be the only way to teach it to hold itself until morning, for dogs will not usually foul their own bed. Try doing this for a few weeks at a time and then allow it its freedom once more. If it is not cured, then confine it for a while longer and it will soon learn. Confining a terrier overnight is not at all cruel, but is a good way of teaching it to hold itself until let out in the morning.

A spray bottle of water mixed with disinfectant and an old cloth will help keep your carpet clean and fresh during housetraining and, if you are diligent and persistent, will no longer be needed after only a short time. Letting your terrier out after mealtimes and when it has just woken from sleep will also help to teach it to go outside.

While a puppy must learn quickly that messing indoors will bring punishment, it must also learn that going outside to urinate and defecate brings praise and rewards, so never neglect to make a fuss of your dog, playing with it and rewarding it whenever it does the correct thing. This same principle applies to the whole training programme. Remember always to make the training sessions exciting and full of fun, keeping them short and filled with praise and rewards. This will build up a dog's confidence and will make it eager to please, for dogs love nothing more than their master's attention and once they realise that obedience to commands brings that attention, and plenty of it, then training will become much easier as the sessions continue.

'Sit.' A fell terrier pup. Training begins as soon as you get your new puppy home.

Training a puppy to sit is child's play. Call the youngster to you and make a fuss of it. While standing still, simply push down gently on its back end and command it to 'sit', praising it while it is still in this position and then playing little games with it afterwards. Repeat the lesson a few times, but do not allow the pup to get bored and thus fed up, and then leave off for a while, keeping the sessions short but frequent, and you may be surprised how quickly it learns.

Getting a young dog to lie down, is also simple enough. Firstly, get it to sit down and then gently pull out the front legs while carefully pressing down on the shoulders until it is in the correct position. Then, once again, give lots of praise while it remains lying down, playing games in order to make the session great fun while maintaining the short but frequent, method. Again, it will not be long before your young trainee is catching on to what is required of it and by now the bonding process will be growing much stronger and the puppy will be assuming its position of submission to its master, particularly when you act quickly and firmly to check any wrong behaviour, which could easily develop into bad habits in the future.

'Sit, stay.'

'Lie down, stay.'

Training the youngster to stay is a little more difficult, but you will soon master it. After getting your puppy in the sitting position, put your hand in front of its face while commanding it to 'stay' in a firm tone of voice, remaining close to it at first and repeating the command frequently. If the puppy moves, which it will usually do far more often than not, make sure you put it back in the sitting position and repeat the 'stay' command. Keep it short, commanding it to stay for only a few seconds at a time in the beginning, then stretching out the time periods to as long as you require as your dog learns and progresses. Make sure that you praise it while it is still in the 'stay' position, but do not reward it after it has moved, which will defeat the object of the exercise. Once it has mastered the 'sit, stay' command, then you can move on to the 'lie down, stay' command.

Lead training is very easy indeed. It can be done in the home and around the garden long before it is inoculated and is so simple I hardly need to describe it. Attach the puppy's collar and allow the puppy to become familiar with it which it will do in no time at all. Do not have the collar so loose that it can either get a paw stuck under it or get it off by slipping it over its head. I also never leave collars on during the night or at other times when they are alone, until the pups get used to them. (Indeed, I never leave collars on generally, for they make an awful mess of the fur around the neck.) And do not have them so tight that the pup is struggling to breathe. Attach the lead and allow the pup to walk around with it for a few minutes before taking hold of it and gently pulling it in the direction you want it to go until it begins walking with you. Make the walks short at first and it will not be long before the puppy is pulling you along. Then it is time to begin training it to heel. Simply jerk the pup back to your side every time it pulls you, commanding it to 'heel' and praising it when it walks by your side. Keep it on a short lead and be persistent. It may take a while before your pup stops taking you for a walk, but the rewards are well worth it.

'Come', 'sit', 'lie down', 'stay' and 'heel' are all basic lessons that will help teach a puppy submission to its master and will help it to learn obedience – a vital quality for the working terrier. If a terrier is just taken out of its kennel, put on couples, taken to an earth and entered, then afterwards put back on couples, taken back to its kennel and put away again, what a miserable life it will have. It is far better to allow it to run free and burn off its excess energy while out at exercise every day, and to have it loose while out hunting, allowing it to use its nose to discover all the delightful scents to be found out in the countryside. For a terrier to do this, it must be trained at least to a basic standard, for it must have learned discipline if it is to know what is acceptable and what is unacceptable for it to hunt. If it has not learned discipline, then controlling it while out at exercise and, more importantly, while out in the hunting field, will be very difficult indeed and may lead to considerable embarrassment as your dog runs riot, completely ignoring your cries for it to return.

One of the most important aspects of a dog's training, and the part you especially have to get right, is stock-breaking. Whether you will be hunting rats, rabbits, foxes, hares or mink (or all of them), it is absolutely essential that your terriers be fully broken to all farm livestock. Stock-breaking should naturally begin with cats, for they are frequently around and are easily found, for there is generally either one around your own house or at a neighbour's.

Keeping the youngster on a short lead, simply allow it to see the cat at close range, so that it also gets a whiff of its scent, and, in a very firm voice, command it to 'leave' while jerking it away, giving it a slap on the backside if it attempts to go after it. Repeat the lesson frequently. If you can get your hands on an old hunting whip or you have a long leather lead, then cracking it on the ground a couple of feet in front of the young dog while repeating the command to 'leave' works wonders and will help instil the lesson very quickly and very effectively indeed. If you have a cat around the home, or a member of your family is willing to help, then let the pup spend some time around the home with it. Some cats will spit fire and fury at the stranger, while others may be enticed to play with it. However you do it, it is extremely important to teach a terrier to leave cats well alone, as they are often to be found out in the countryside, skulking in coverts, hunting mice or stalking birds, or even below ground in a fox earth. If you will be hunting rats around a farmyard, then it is even more important that your terrier be steady to the feline species, for many cats frequent farmyards and it does not give a good impression to a farmer if your dog attacks or even kills his animals.

So be diligent when it comes to breaking a young dog to cats. I once watched two of my terriers (Ghyll and Mist) hunting keenly across a hillside, heading for a large patch of bramble thickets where I had just spotted a cat skulking in the undergrowth. Both had been broken to cats, but my heart was still in my mouth as they approached and, as the puss broke cover, I was extremely relieved to see both terriers pick up its scent and turn away immediately, totally uninterested. The effort required to teach steadiness to a puppy is well worth it when you get results of this kind.

Stock-breaking to farm livestock is so simple that it is a crime to neglect this essential part of a youngster's training programme. Sheep, cattle, horses, hens, ducks and geese are all readily found and the same method used for breaking to cats can be employed. Repeating these lessons regularly is vital, and the more a young working dog is around these animals, becoming familiar with the sight and scent of them, the better. For they must quickly learn that it is unacceptable to chase them, thus guaranteeing that you can trust them while they are loose above ground.

I cannot stress enough how important it is that these lessons be thoroughly instilled in a youngster *before* its entering programme begins so that they can then be reinforced as you encounter livestock whilst out hunting. Sheep may be feeding in a large bracken bed and may flee from a terrier which is working the covert, often startling the dog and offering a temptation to chase which some will find very hard to resist.

On several occasions I have watched my terriers while hunting rabbits, hares or foxes through reedbeds and bracken, suddenly come upon a sheep which, typically, has reacted hysterically and has ran off, almost shouting 'chase me', but the dogs, thankfully, have remained steady. It gives a lot of peace of mind to know that your workers will remain steady when encountering livestock. In fact, no matter how steady they are, mine have a refresher course every summer just before hunting begins again in September, as well as reminders throughout the season. I find that this method works extremely well and is more than worth the effort involved.

To recap, keep the training sessions short, make them happy, fun times and always give plenty of praise and reward. Be diligent when it comes to breaking dogs to livestock and, while out at exercise, if you see a cat or come across livestock, then reinforce the lesson.

Remember, spoilt dogs are like spoilt children, unpleasant company and a source of great embarrassment, so make sure your dogs know who is the boss and you will enjoy their company and their work for years to come.

Pep with her pups (Judy on right). Notice how well broken she is to cats.

5

Obtaining Permission and Entering the Young Terrier

With the youngster settled in and its socialising and training well along, the bond between dog and master firmly established, it is now time to begin entering the young terrier to its traditional quarry, the rat, rabbit and fox. Badgers and otters are no longer on the list, but mink can and should also be hunted. Although they are beautiful, graceful creatures, they are ruthless killers whose predatory antics on our riverbanks have caused serious devastation to our native wildlife and they need to be tightly controlled, if not eliminated, for they are alien to the British countryside and have no natural predators.

However it is the rat, the rabbit and the fox that traditionally concern the worker of terriers, though some may also hunt hares with their earth dogs, as I do, as this can really help teach a youngster to use its nose, thus helping it to learn how to find in a huge, deep earth or a large bracken bed or bramble covert. I have found that the best finders are those which have learned how to use their nose as youngsters.

Before it is possible to begin the entering process, however, it is essential that you obtain permission from farmers. Unfortunately, this is not always easy; in fact, it can often be very difficult indeed. Although society is less concerned with dress than before, if you go to the door of a farmer or landowner wearing jeans and a sweatshirt, looking unshaven, and ask for permission to hunt over their land, you will more often than not go away from the interview disappointed to say the least. It is far better to go dressed smartly, in shirt and tie, with a neat pair of trousers and shiny shoes. True, farmyards can be muddy places at times and you will no doubt get your shoes a little dirty, but it will be well worth it in the end if you obtain some good land which has a healthy population of rabbits and some good coverts where foxes may be found.

Being well dressed is essential and it may also improve your chances if you have a few business cards printed (these can be done very cheaply on computers nowadays), advertising the fact that you are offering a free pest control service which the farmer can only benefit from. Remember to smile and be friendly, though never smug or over-confident as you will give the impression of arrogance. Be chatty. Ask the farmer about his stock and show him that you fully support farmers in their plight today as agriculture continues to suffer great hardships, and make it clear that you are providing a service. Make it clear that you will respect his livestock, that your dogs are stock steady, and that you will take great care with his walls and fences, assuring him that you will repair any damage you or your dogs may cause, however unlikely. Dogs can knock a stone or two off the top of a wall when scrambling over, or you could disturb them with your boots. Doing on-the-spot repairs will go a long way to ensuring that you enjoy the farmer's favour and keep the land for years to come.

If you have the time to spare, you may also mention that you are available to help out for a few hours during busier times on the agricultural calendar, or you may offer to do one or two fence repairs if you come across any damage on his land. These are tried and tested methods which get results and, provided you are well dressed, polite and respectful, you will soon find yourself with enough permission to begin hunting, though, of course, it is important that you maintain that permission if you are to enjoy the land's bounty well into the future.

Now and then (it does not have to be on a regular basis) offer a little help around the place and, if you see him when you are out hunting, make a little time to stop and chat. You may even decide to call in with the odd bottle of wine to thank him for allowing you to hunt on his property. When Tim, a good friend of mine, acquired some prime hunting grounds in Staffordshire a few years ago, obtaining permission from the head keeper of the large estate, he would take the keeper a bottle of whisky at least once a year to show his gratitude, and always make sure that he called in to spend a bit of time chatting whenever he was down that way. It was a certain way of maintaining that prime permission.

If the farmer is ever in trouble and needs your help, then do your best to provide it, even if it means less time spent hunting. Sometimes emergencies do crop up and you must be willing to drop everything in order to provide much-needed assistance, although these occasions are very rare indeed. I can remember one such occasion.

We had enjoyed a hard day's hunting up in the high hills which tower above our smoky little industrial northern town, which huddles on the plains below the rising swell of the western Pennines. We had not gone up into the rough, windblown Pennines, but instead had climbed into the tall green hills east of the wide plains, fertile and less harassed by the elements, where we had been hunting rabbits and foxes. We had checked the huge rockpiles at the old quarry and, finding them blank, had moved on up to the crags where, again, nothing could be found. We had tried the numerous stone drains, ancient and often dry, but again the quarry proved elusive. So we had to content ourselves with numerous runs at rabbits, a couple of which were successful, and a single rat taken as we headed down from the high ground on our way back home. We had been out since dawn and so were tired and more than ready to put our feet up.

We had to pass through the farmyard however, and there the farmer met us, asking for our help as one of his neighbour's cows had fallen into a ditch and could not get up. A chilled beck runs through the bottom of this ditch, draining the pastures of the icy water which seeps down from the bleak, high tops. The cow had been there for some time now and found it impossible to get up. I went for the cow's owner, and it took all four of us, with a lot of effort and not a little time, to get the cow to her feet and out of the cold water, up the steep bank and back onto level ground. We had to remain there for some time while she steadied herself until her strength and balance returned and it was at long last safe to leave her to rejoin the herd.

Both farmers were most grateful and this episode has helped me keep my permission for many years, something I am extremely grateful for. I have taken many foxes from this place and its coverts and earths are well used. It also continues to hold a few rats – though not many after my dogs had found and accounted for a good number of them – quite a number of rabbits and the odd hare or two, so it is land well worth having.

Gaining permission to decent land is absolutely essential and may be a little easier to obtain these days, at least in some cases, with the hunting community so openly giving its support to farmers, and vice versa, all standing together against the escalating attacks on the countryside and real country life. So, when asking for permission, do not be afraid to tell the farmer of your support, as this may endear you to him and may help swing the balance in your favour. And remember, make sure you realise the importance of maintaining that permission. Respect livestock and property and always show proper care for the countryside by taking your litter home with you and, after digging out a ferret or a terrier, making sure that you back-fill properly and leave the area as neat and tidy as you possibly can. It may also help to join a recognised terrier club, one which has a rescue service, just in case your dog should ever get into trouble while working below ground. You can then assure the farmer that you will strictly abide by the club code of conduct. Permission on good land is well worth the effort it takes to obtain and maintain it.

Once permission has been acquired (something that can be done even before you have bought your puppy, or while it is being trained to a standard of obedience which will help you to control it out in the hunting field) it is time to begin the entering process, which will see the puppy transformed, after a great deal of time and effort, into an adult working terrier. In order to do this in the most effective manner possible, it is best to allow your puppy to observe an adult, mature worker in action, for this is the best method of beginning the entering process and it will unquestionably produce the fastest and the best results. It is the same principle as an apprentice learning from his master, a pupil from his teacher. In order to do this, you may need to team up with someone who already has working dogs, if you can. If not, then it may be necessary to purchase an entered terrier that can teach your youngster the art of hunting above and below ground. Of course, a terrier worked alone, if it is bred right with a good inherited hunting instinct, will learn what is required of it in time, but it will take much longer to catch on than the terrier shown the ropes by an adult worker. Likewise, two youngsters brought on together will help and encourage one another and will progress faster than a lone trainee. So it may well be worth investing in two puppies, as I have said, rather than just the one. Not only are they good company for each other, but they will also make better progress and enjoy better results while out hunting.

Breaking a young terrier to ferrets is obviously essential if you will be using them for hunting rabbits and rats. It is especially important to use ferrets when bringing a young terrier on as bolting rats and rabbits are good at 'geeing' up a terrier and getting it excited. Getting a terrier familiar with ferrets is best done when it is a young pup so that it is well used to them by the time work begins, for it must quickly decide whether what is emerging from a hole is a rat or a ferret (or a rabbit or a ferret), and it must be able to act quickly enough to avoid killing or seriously injuring its ally. This can only

No, he isn't here!

They found their fox a few feet further on, skulking under the stone piles.

be achieved by getting a terrier very familiar with the sight and scent of your ferrets and by teaching it to leave them well alone. Using ferrets to test the courage of a young terrier is both cruel and unnecessary. Reject any advice to engage in this barbaric method of testing guts in a terrier, for they will enter to their legitimate quarry when they are good and ready without these cruel, Victorian methods.

The first six months of a terrier's life are best spent having lots of fun while also being instructed. By the time a puppy reaches six months of age it should be ready to begin the entering process, one that may continue for the next eighteen months or so – or even longer in some cases. Some learn very slowly indeed, especially an immature terrier, which can be a great source of irritation to the impatient owner during entering, driving him mad with frustration until they suddenly blossom into extremely reliable workers once maturity comes, maybe as late as the latter part of its second season. By the time a young entry reaches the age of six months, it should have been well drilled in basic obedience and should be broken to all farm livestock and socialised with other dogs too. It should therefore be ready to begin learning its trade.

It is best to become well acquainted with the land first, before you begin hunting it, so that you can locate any badger setts which may be encountered by a young, curious terrier, which may become lost or badly mauled in them, possibly spoiling it for work in the future, not to mention breaking the law in the process. So locate any setts quickly and stay clear of those areas so as to avoid any accidents. You can also become familiar with the best-looking coverts to try and the best spots for rabbits, thus ensuring plenty of fun and excitement for your pup, for a young and inexperienced terrier can soon become disheartened when working blank spots.

Rabbits are the quarry you should start a terrier to and this is easily done. Take your puppy to a good spot where there are plenty of rabbits, preferably during the early morning, or the evening if this is a better time for you, and encourage it to chase and hunt them. If one goes into a warren, encourage the pup to sniff the hole but guard against too much encouragement, as this can cause false marking. Once you have put the terrier on a lead and have pegged it down, net the holes and enter your ferret (remember, you are there to carry out pest control as well as to enter your terrier, and, believe me, rabbit damage to pasture can be horrendous where they thrive in large numbers). Then, once the rabbit is secured in the net and has been despatched quickly and humanely, allow your pup to 'rag' the carcass, teasing it by dragging it around and shaking it. At other times, allow the youngster to chase bolting rabbits (it may even succeed in catching one or two) while continuing to net and despatch others, thus keeping the farmer happy and your larder topped up with first-class ferret and dog meat, and maybe the odd rabbit stew for the family.

Encourage your puppy to hunt the line of a rabbit's scent and entice it to enter the undergrowth, whether it be reedbeds, bracken or bramble thickets, in search of them. Once they begin finding and flushing them out into the open, you will have great satisfaction in knowing that your young entry is really beginning to catch on and is making excellent progress. It will not be long before the youngster

Drawing for scent above ground.

begins marking occupied rabbit warrens too, saving you a lot of unnecessary ferreting time and building a foundation which will help it to mark and find in fox earths when it begins work below ground, the true work of the terrier.

Once it has caught on and is eagerly hunting and chasing rabbits, entering cover and seeking them, it will not be long, especially in a country well populated with foxes, before they catch a whiff of their scent and follow it eagerly, finding and flushing its fox out into the open and giving you a spectacular view. It is not desirable for a terrier to face a fox in an earth until it is at least twelve months old, preferably fourteen or even fifteen months, especially if it is sensitive or immature, but it is impossible for the young entry which hunts rabbits above ground in the type of country foxes favour, not to come across the latter at some time and hunt them long before it is ready to face them underground. My young terriers have usually found and flushed many foxes from undergrowth long before starting their earth work. If you have an experienced terrier that

Emerging from an empty earth.

can run an earth first, or tell you that it is unoccupied by its lack of interest, then you may run a youngster to ground as early as six months or so, but if not keep it out of earths until it is twelve months, in case it receives a bad bite and is either put off its work, possibly for good, or becomes too hard, constantly closing with its fox and taking punishment nearly every time it goes to ground and having to be rested up for the next two or three weeks until its wounds heal. If you avoid overfacing a young entry with work it cannot yet cope with, then it will mature into a good, sensible worker which can be taken out week in, week out throughout the season.

Rats are only small creatures and no match for a terrier, but they can bite savagely. A young terrier can easily be put off hunting and tackling them if it receives a bad bite too early in its career, so avoid hunting rats until your youngster is at least eight months old and then one of the most exciting of hunting exploits can begin at last. Ferrets are the best method of bolting them, though they can also be smoked out of their lairs, and they are easily found on riverbanks, by the sides of brooks, in stone walls, around the farmyard and especially amongst rubbish on a tip. Get your terrier to stand still near to one of the holes and wait for the action to begin. It has to be said that several terriers are far more effective at this game than one on its own. So if you are going on ratting expeditions, it is best to team up with someone else who owns working dogs. Rats bolt at an incredible speed and one dog, especially if it is a novice, can be very ineffective when several are bolting in all different directions, but a small team of terriers – at least two, though three or more can be much more effective – can achieve some serious pest control. I have also taken huge numbers of rats with a mixed group of terriers, lurchers and greyhounds.

Testing the air around the earth's entrance, terriers will soon learn to mark an earth as occupied or otherwise.

Bess had enjoyed a short career as a track racing greyhound and came to me after she had grown too old to be competitive, though she was still only around four or five years old, and I took her up into the hills in order to improve her fitness in readiness for the coming season. I spent long hours out in the countryside in those days and was on my way home as the sun began to sink behind the darkening bulk of the rising moorland to the west on that late summer evening. On the edge of our estate, bordering the countryside, were several allotments and it was out in the field, close to these pens that I noticed movement in the damp grass. I crept closer, with Bess at my side, and watched as a large rat drank from a little puddle which had settled in a cow's hoofmark. When it saw me, it scurried for cover at the allotments. I loosed Bess who was on it in no time, very quickly despatching it, though not before it had bitten her savagely, leaving a scar that she carried for the rest of her days. So it is not just terriers that make good ratters, for Bess took several more during her lifetime, although obviously terriers are far more agile and can quickly catch bolting rats.

By the time a young terrier has completed its first year of life, it should be hunting rabbits keenly from cover and marking occupied warrens accurately. It should be taking rats fearlessly by now, and, marking holes expertly. And it will no doubt have discovered the delights of finding and flushing foxes from undergrowth and hunting their line eagerly. At this age, unless your terrier is still rather immature or very sensitive, it will be ready to begin working below ground and, again, is best entered to fox by allowing it to watch an adult, mature worker in action.

When entering a terrier to an earth, encourage it to search through the dark tunnels with a few soft words, avoiding too much encouragement which can make it false mark, even baying below ground when the earth is empty. These are bad habits that are extremely difficult to eradicate, so it is best not to allow them to develop in the first place, which can only be done by being patient and allowing the young entry to progress at its own pace.

Never put two male terriers to ground together as they may begin fighting. You can then do nothing to stop them, and serious injury, or even death, may result. If two bitches, or a dog and a bitch, get on well enough and are well acquainted with one another, then it is good to allow both to go to ground together until they have a better idea of what is required of them. Then only one terrier should be put to ground at any one time; once both have bolted a few foxes from earths, then it is time to stop putting them both to ground together, working them single-handed from then on. This is best done as soon as possible because they can soon become used to each other's support and may not work a fox properly when they suddenly find they are alone. So separate them as soon as possible, when they have learned to find and bolt foxes from below ground.

It is good to net the bolt hole and quickly despatch your fox humanely, shooting it as it bolts, or taking it with lurchers, so that the youngsters can taste the carcass. This will help build their confidence and will also help them to continue making progress. If the local farming community has not suffered any fox predation during recent weeks, or foxes have been a little thin on the ground, it does no harm at all to allow some foxes to run for another day. In fact, it really excites a terrier when it bolts a fox from an earth and hunts its hot scent across the rough ground above, speaking keenly to its line and returning only when it has checked and cannot pick up the scent again. Despite what you may have read or been told, terriers do not need to 'rag' a fox's carcass every time in order to progress in its work. Even if a terrier hardly ever tastes a carcass, it will still hunt foxes above and below ground efficiently. When terriers were used for digging foxes for their fur, they never tasted the carcass for fear of damaging the coat, yet they continued to work foxes without any detrimental effects on their abilities. Even if the fox is allowed to run at the end of a dig, if a terrier is allowed to give chase and hunt it, it will in no way be disheartened, but will thoroughly enjoy itself, delighting in the chase.

When it comes to digging foxes from earths, which will be necessary where they are causing damage to a farmer's livestock, first

Fell terriers drawing for foxes through the heather, a good covert for Reynard.

enter an experienced terrier after blocking all the holes except the one you are using. Give it a little time to settle down in one spot before proceeding with the dig. You should have purchased a locator by now and, as long as you follow the instructions provided, you should not have any problems with it. Some people I know will not use them in rock, for fear of the collar catching between two rocks and hanging the dog but this is extremely rare, and your terrier is far more likely to die from being knocked over.

You may wish to enter your youngster at this point and it should soon find the fox being keenly bayed by its ally. With this method, however, the youngster, in its excitement, may push the other terrier closer to the fox, which will punish it unmercifully. I have also found that, if the youngster has a stronger personality and is more excitable, it will push its way past the other dog if there is enough room in the tunnel. I find the best way is to dig to the experienced worker alone, and then replace it with the young entry for the last few minutes of the dig. Once you have humanely dealt with your

Where is he? Mist looking for her fox which she knows is somewhere in this huge borran.

fox, you can allow both to taste the carcass together. If you are allowing the fox to run for another day, then allow both to give chase and encourage them on as they hunt its scent. This will really help a young terrier to make progress.

If you have no access to an experienced worker, then all you can do is put your terrier to ground and allow it a few minutes to settle with its fox in the same way, then begin digging. Being in-experienced, your terrier may emerge after twenty minutes or so, so encourage it to go back, but do not be disheartened if it will not. Simply replace it with the other youngster, if you are hunting two, and dig to that one instead. Again, it may emerge and refuse to go back – this is normal in a youngster with little experience, so do not despair. Unblock the holes and keep the pair by your side while remaining as quiet as possible. Often, the fox will emerge and you can then encourage your terriers to chase and hunt it, generating as much excitement as you possibly can. As your charges mature, they will settle to their work and begin staying until they are dug out.

If a fox will not bolt from an earth that is undiggable, then getting it out can be a problem. Once a terrier knows you are digging to it, it will be encouraged to stay with its fox, so try calling it out. If it still remains with its fox, (which, quite frankly, it probably will do), then I find the best way of getting it to emerge is to move well away from the earth and remain silent. The terrier may then come out to see what is going on, although, from my experience, you may have to wait for several hours. A terrier should stay with its fox when being dug to, but it should have the intelligence to come off it once it has realised that nothing is happening. Not for me the terrier which will stay till Doomsday when the earth is impossible to dig. In this situation, the old fell huntsmen would always have a terrier which could finish a fox underground.

Once a youngster has replaced the older terrier a few times at the end of a dig, spending a little more time with its fox each time, it is then time to allow it to go to ground alone at the start of the dig, and to stay the whole time. If it does not stay, do not worry. As it gains more experience and grows in maturity, it will soon settle properly to its work and, usually towards the end of its second season, will become a good, reliable worker – though some do not settle properly until as late as their third season, reaching their peak during their fourth or fifth season.

Always encourage your terrier in its work and guard against giving it large tasks to perform too early. Rabbits can easily be tackled by a terrier as young as four months, though it is much better to wait until it is six months old, letting it hunt them in cover and gently encouraging it to mark warrens, teasing its instincts for entering dark passages underground. This will teach it to use its nose and will help it when rat hunting begins at eight months (no younger, for you do not want it to receive a bad bite that may put it off its work). By the time it reaches its first year, it will probably have found, flushed and hunted several foxes from coverts and may be ready for earth work to begin. Let it find and bolt a few foxes before beginning to dig to it, and allow it to progress at its own pace. Do not over-encourage and never lose your temper. Sticking to these guidelines will help your terrier to make good progress and you will then go on to enjoy some cracking hunting for years to come.

Terriers are naturally drawn to dark passages underground.

6

The Terrier Pack

Terriers, strictly speaking, are not pack animals, though they were once very popular as such, especially during the early part of the twentieth century when they were used for hunting almost anything that moved. Sir Jocelyn Lucas, author of *Hunt and Working Terriers*, ran on a pack of Sealyham terriers during those long-lost times when it was still possible to work with pedigree breeds of terrier (Bedlingtons and borders are still worked to this day, but few of the other breeds are). Major Doig ran on a pack of fox terriers in Africa and some of the old fell terrier breeders, many of whom were instrumental in the creation of the pedigree lakeland terrier, often hunted a pack of them at all sorts of quarry, mainly during the summer months, when the fell packs were enjoying their rest during the off-season.

Terrier packs still exist today, and are used for hunting a variety of quarry. Members of the Scottish Hill Packs Association hunt a terrier pack up in the Highlands of Scotland, and they are used for fox control. Keith Francis hunts a pack of Lucas terriers, a breed which is rapidly rising in popularity, at rabbits and mink, and there are one or two Plummer terrier packs around, for this rather attractive breed packs quite well (though some can be aggressive with other dogs), probably because of the fairly recent inclusion of beagle blood in its make-up, something which gives it a good nose as well as packing ability.

I have been involved in hunting a pack of terriers for almost two decades now, though the numbers have fluctuated from just two members to eight or even ten at times. It was not just terriers in the pack either, for lurchers and greyhounds were for some time part of our team, and we have enjoyed great success with rats, rabbits, hares, foxes and mink, with the odd hunt or two on grey squirrels. There is no uniformity in a pack of this kind – they are a rough and ready bunch of fell and Jack Russell terriers, mongrelly lurchers and ex-track racing greyhounds, but who cares! Uniformity is for those

Hunting through heather and rock.

with their proud packs of hounds. I go for working ability every time and, once members of a pack get to know each other and begin working as a team, gaining experience and assessing each others strengths and weaknesses, they become unbeatable out in the field.

More recently, a brace of teckels (long-haired dachshunds) have joined my small team of terriers, owned by John Hill, a teacher from Ramsbottom in Lancashire, and we have been enjoying some superb hunting as a result. Teckels certainly have good noses, but they do not stand up too well to the bad weather we suffer in the north of England.

If you are interested in hunting a terrier pack, you can do one of two things to get started. If you have enough room for a small kennel block and the money to fill it, then you could buy in a few terriers, preferably including one or two which are already entered, just to start you off. Alternatively, you could get together with a friend or two and hunt your different charges together, in the same manner as a trencher-fed* farmer's pack used to be managed in the old days, with one person acting as huntsman and the others acting as whippers-in. This will keep your costs down considerably. For most of the time, this is how I have managed to hunt a pack, and it is

* Hounds kennelled separately at different locations and brought together for hunting only. This is a popular way of hunting in rural Ireland.

an excellent way of seeing a team of dogs at work without the expense of keeping them all.

Of course, you may prefer to own and work your own dogs, but doing it in this way does have its drawbacks. Hunting two, three, or even four terriers by yourself is extremely rewarding, and these numbers are not too difficult to handle provided they have been well schooled in basic obedience. But I would not be inclined to work larger numbers by myself, as control may be difficult to say the least. If you have a friend or two who can act as whips to your little pack, then the hunting of larger numbers of terriers together is made much easier and will give you the confidence of knowing that there are others there to help out should anything go wrong – and, believe me, things can go wrong from time to time.

Basic obedience training, including breaking to cats and farm live-stock, is essential for any working terrier, but even more so for those that will make up a pack, because if one weakens and gives chase to a fast-fleeing sheep there is every chance that all will be inclined to join in. Afterwards, you will find it very difficult indeed, what-ever the corrective methods you use, to trust those pack members again, and this distrust can ruin a day's hunting, for it destroys your peace of mind and has an unsettling affect, on both yourself and your pack. So school pack members hard to leave livestock alone, giving a little extra instruction when it comes to sheep, for it is often the way these silly creatures behave that weakens a terrier's resolve and entices it to give chase.

A pack of game terriers is very effective indeed when it comes to rat hunting and will soon become adept at picking up the bolting rodents, for few will escape their attentions. A good little pack is worth its weight in gold, for it is far more effective than any pest controller's poisons and will soon dramatically reduce rat numbers when the pack pays a visit to a place that is troubled by them. Ferrets or smoke can be used to bolt rats, and you may decide to use ferrets for bolting rabbits for the pack to hunt as well, although this is not always necessary. Once a pack has settled, having got to know how each individual works, who is the most reliable at finding etc. they can soon become very adept at catching rabbits, especially when they hide in cover. Terriers are extremely quick off the mark and can speedily snap up a rabbit which has bolted in front of them after they have worked out its line and eventually found where it is lying up in the undergrowth.

When carrying out rat and rabbit control it pays dividends to work the trouble spots on a regular basis and you can help reduce

Mist emerging from a borran earth after showing a lot of interest. She found her fox at another spot further along the fellside.

their numbers dramatically if you are diligent. However, when it comes to the hunting of foxes, it does not pay to visit an area that is inhabited by them too often, for they will suddenly disappear and no longer use their earths and coverts if you do so. Foxes are mysterious creatures and have a knack of evading capture, so you need to keep the element of surprise on your side if you are going to be effective at hunting and controlling them. So do not hunt coverts and earths too regularly. I have found that visiting them once a month gives the foxes the confidence to keep the earths and coverts in use. Sometimes it may be necessary to visit once a fortnight, especially at lambing time, but that is the limit for you will simply drive them away and, unless you lamp them at night with dog or gun, you will not find them.

Deer can be a problem to the huntsman of a pack of terriers as these dogs will hunt their scent as keenly as that of rabbit or fox. I was out recently with a brace of terriers and on two separate occasions, while looking for foxes, we came across deer; the dogs put their noses to the ground and hunted the line excitedly. But you can never get close enough to deer to be able to break your terriers to them, so all you can do is call your terriers off, or whip them off if possible, plainly showing your disapproval and firmly warning them against this unlawful pursuit with a shout of '*leave*' which you can only hope they will not block out. If I had had several terriers out with me that day, I would have found it extremely difficult, if not impossible, to control them. As it was, with just the brace, I was easily able to call them off and soon had them under control, thankfully. This is another reason not to hunt too many terriers at one time. Just hunt the number you are comfortable with and feel you can handle.

Using a whistle or, better still, a hunting horn, can also help to control a pack once they have got used to the various commands, and is also useful for bringing the pack out of cover when it is time to move on to the next covert. If the pack gets well ahead of you on a hot scent, then it is vital that you keep in touch with them so that they do not lose their way and fail to find you again. Blowing on the horn once or twice will tell them of your whereabouts, and they will easily find you again. I have lost touch with my terriers several times and, before I began using the horn, I failed to find one or two members – though fortunately I was hunting locally and they found their way home safely. It was this that made me decide to use a hunting horn, and they work very effectively indeed, for terriers can hear them at very long distances. Also, if a pack is going away on a scent in a direction you do not wish them to go in, then blowing on the horn can get them to lift their heads and return to you.

For much of the year, foxes spend their time above ground and shelter in much the same type of cover as rabbits, though I have

Checking for scent.

70

'Peep-O'! Foxes will often lie close in deep heather such as this.

found that brambles and bracken are particular favourites. So it is inevitable that you will come across them during your hunting forays, and your pack will hunt them eagerly indeed. I do not know what it is about fox scent, but it seems to drive terriers wild, and they will hunt them really keenly, often without even knowing just what it is they are pursuing. More often than not a fox's scent will fizzle out and be lost, the terriers will be unable to pick it up again, but the fox will sometimes prove a little unadventurous and will go to ground with the pack following. Sometimes he will bolt again and be hunted a while longer, or he will choose a corner and stand his ground. If this is the case, then get the pack out as soon as possible. Only one will actually be up to its fox and the others should soon emerge in search of another way in; this is your chance to get hold of them. You can then decide to try to bolt it again, or you may wish to dig to it, it is entirely up to you, but if a local farmer has been having problems with foxes, it is best either to bolt it to a gun or lurcher or to dig to it and despatch it quickly and humanely. This will keep the farmer happy and may even end his troubles.

Much of this type of hunting, though extremely exciting, is done either in cover or underground and thus little of the work done by the pack members is actually seen. This is when hunting hares comes into its own. Hares are creatures of open spaces and some excellent hunting can be seen as you watch your pack find and chase, yapping for all they are worth as they try in vain to catch their prey – which you can almost hear chuckling to itself as it runs away rather casually, its large ears erect – and then settle to its line when it has gone out of sight. Unless your terriers pack well – which is very unlikely unless they are Plummer terriers or have beagle blood in their recent make-up – then it will not be long before they lose the scent. All may not be lost, however, especially if you have seen where the hare has gone, for you can then 'lift' your pack and cast them, getting them back onto the line as you do your best to keep the hunt going. Though it is generally a fruitless pursuit, it can help your terriers to learn to work hard at owning a line and, at the same time, will give you much pleasure as you watch them work at close proximity.

Grey squirrels are often referred to, a little unkindly perhaps, as 'tree rats' because of their ability to thrive in large numbers where they have taken over and driven out the once common and very beautiful red squirrel. It is important that they are culled, more especially in areas where their red cousins are trying to make a comeback, and a terrier pack enjoys nothing more than chasing them around the woodland floor and, in conjunction with a gun, which can be used when they get out of the way of the pack by climbing a tree, this can be a very effective means of controlling them.

I was out hunting woodland during the autumn a few years ago with three fell terriers which had been keeping busy attempting to catch rabbits and were now occupied with a red-hot scent which they keenly followed under some thick evergreen bushes. A commotion told me they had found, and a grey squirrel came rushing out from under the bushes and sped across the ground at lightning speed and scrambled up the thick trunk while Rock, Ghyll and Crag followed its line keenly, rushing to the tree and baying loudly for blood. Unbelievably, the squirrel, after reaching certain safety, came back down again and made a bid for open ground once

This rock-pile often holds foxes and is situated near a farm where the occupants often take a heavy toll on the farmer's livestock. There is only one way of shifting foxes from such a place; with working terriers.

more. The dogs went in pursuit immediately and chased it up another tree where, again, it came down and then ran up another tree. I was totally baffled by its behaviour, especially as it could have escaped easily a long time before, but once again it found itself on the woodland floor and this time it ran under some bushes, where Crag was quickly upon it, putting an end to its crazy behaviour.

On another occasion, I was out with a brace of fell terriers, Mist and Fell, when Mist marked a small covert before entering, baying and flushing a squirrel which found itself nowhere near any trees. It came flying out of that covert while Fell joined Mist inside, and came bounding past me. It had obviously seen me, but was not put off its course at all, so I was then treated to some excellent hunting as they followed its scent across the wet ground, through dead bracken stalks which were laid flat in places after the recent heavy rains, and into a small woodland on the hillside, where it eventually got away safely.

When putting a terrier pack together, you need to be cautious. I would not advise that two dogs be worked together unless, first, they get on well, and, second, there is no chance of them getting to ground together. This means getting to know your country extremely well indeed so that you know where all the earths are and can avoid that area just to make sure that no accidents happen. Bitches can sometimes take a real dislike to one another, too, so be careful. Make sure that all the pack members get on well and then they will concentrate on the job in hand instead of settling old scores.

Spectacular hunting will be enjoyed if you take on a terrier pack, whether at your own expense or in the manner of the trencher-fed pack, and, provided they are well behaved and steady to livestock, they will help to carry out some first-class pest control. Nothing can compare with seeing a young terrier becoming a useful member of an efficient pack; it is the stuff a terrierman's dreams are made of.

I can remember one particular hunting day that stands out more than most, for it was the day that Ghyll, a terrier that went on to become the best I have ever owned, had his first unaided find. Most of the leaves had been shaken from the trees, and that autumn Ghyll had joined the terrier pack and was enjoying his first season. Rock, Crag and Bella had been extremely busy finding and flushing hares, foxes and rabbits, with Ghyll joining in the hunt much more keenly as the autumn months progressed. As yet, however he had failed to do the finding for himself. We were hunting the lowlands, where quite large woodlands flourished. My little pack hunted eagerly for scent. They busily chased squirrels up trees and hunted the odd rabbit.

We entered Linnet Wood and all the terriers got their noses down and hunted keenly. Rock, as usual, soon found a rabbit, which the pack chased and hunted, and which eventually went to ground in a hole under a tree. The pack soon returned to the wood and I then noticed that Ghyll had wandered off by himself, a problem which is regularly encountered, as terriers do not pack very well. I could see the others hunting the top half of the wood and soon discovered that Ghyll had found what must have been a good scent and had followed it down to the bottom part of the wood, where a lot of thick undergrowth grew, and where I could now hear him baying as he came towards me through the numerous uneven lines of trees. It was very difficult to see exactly what he was chasing and I had a very brief glimpse of something which looked about the size of a terrier. All the pack then came together and I had a spectacular view of them as they hunted its line across the rough ground, twisting and turning through the trees until they checked and eventually lost it somewhere on the waterlogged pasture at the far end of the wood, failing to pick up the line again. To this day I do not know what it was that Ghyll found, 'either a large hare or a fox' is what I wrote in my journal, but it did not really matter, for he was at last catching on and was now beginning to find his place as a useful member of the pack. It was to be the beginning of great things from Ghyll and from that day on he never looked back.

Keeping your terrier pack fit during the season is obviously essential if they are to give their best and to have enough stamina to

Rock and Ghyll on the top of Loughrigg, watching out for the Coniston pack.

cope with a long day's hunting in often freezing conditions. It is desirable to rest your terriers the day after hunting, but a decent walk is necessary on all other non-hunting days if they are to remain in tip-top condition. Over an hour would be best, but it is not always possible to give them this long due to work or family commitments, so not less than half an hour on a field where they can have a good run around should help to keep them fit enough for their busy work schedule.

During the summer off-season, particularly if you will not be hunting mink, it is far less important to maintain peak fitness, though a decent walk most days will prevent them from becoming bored and potentially troublesome, for boredom may cause fighting as they take their frustration out on others. Walking them will also help them to settle at night, something that is especially important if they are kennelled outside. Of course, if they are enjoying more leisure time and less exercise, then remember to cut their food portions down a little too, or they will run to fat very quickly and it can be hard work getting it off when hunting time comes around again.

If you do rest them during the summer months, then make sure that, as the new season approaches, you steadily increase their exercise periods so that they are reasonably fit by the time hunting starts again. I always include some roadwork at this time, as this helps to build muscle and hardens the pads, thus equipping them well for work in thick coverts and rocks.

It is essential that you keep your pack members in good condition during the hunting season in particular, as this will help them to give of their best out in the field and will also enable them to stand up to the rigours of the hunt and prolong their working life. It is no good having a terrier that is burnt out after six or seven seasons when you could be enjoying its work for upwards of ten or even eleven seasons, a reasonable working lifespan if you look after your terrier properly.

Rock, retired after eleven seasons, is now an ancient veteran at nearly seventeen years of age (at time of writing).

7

Terrier Breeding

If money is a little tight and you wish to increase the number of terriers you keep for working, then breeding your own stock may be the best option available to you. Provided you can afford the stud fee – usually around £50 at the time of writing – this is an excellent way of building a kennel of working terriers and, of course, the best way of giving a fairly large number of terriers the amount of work needed to keep them happy is to work them as a pack. Moreover, there is no better way to build a pack which need to get on well together if they are to work peaceably with one another, than to breed and raise them yourself. Of course, it is the best policy not to have any more than two terriers of the same age, as you could end up with several retired veterans which you are unable to replace until they die. So stagger their ages by starting off with just two and, once they have entered and have a couple of seasons experience behind them, breed and keep a couple more, and so on until you have the numbers you require. One of the advantages of two or three people getting together and forming a little pack to hunt, of course is that you can have pack members of all ages and, once one or two of these are forced into retirement due to old age, they can easily be replaced because the costs are kept down to a minimum.

As I have said, when buying a puppy you should always purchase from a litter bred from good working parents, and the same applies to breeding for yourself. A terrier, dog or bitch, should not be bred from until it has worked for at least two seasons so that it can be fully tested in the field in all sorts of situations, in order to make certain that you produce puppies from the right stuff – good workers. A bitch may have its first season (come on heat) at six months, but it is not ready, emotionally more than physically, to produce puppies, for it is still a baby itself. At twelve months, it is just about to begin its career working foxes below ground and you will have no idea how it will perform. Will it find foxes either above or below ground? Will it work them sensibly, baying steadily and bolting them? If it is a hard terrier, will it deal with a reluctant fox underground without receiving serious injury? Will it stay to a fox until it is dug out? How does it stand up to bitterly cold weather and a long day's hunting? Does it get on well with children and other dogs? These are all questions which need definite answers *before* you breed from a terrier and these answers cannot usually be obtained until it has served for at least two seasons, for a working terrier may not mature properly until late in its second season, when it will be approaching its third year.

So do not be in a hurry to breed from a terrier and *never*, breed for show purposes. This is the scourge of the working terrier world and has been the ruination of many once excellent strains which were famous for their working abilities. I am not condemning terrier shows or showing, for I have been involved in both the running and exhibiting at shows, sometimes with considerable success. It is breeding exclusively for shows that has spelt the end for many once first-class strains of working terrier.

Brian Nuttall, a man who always strives to produce top-quality workers, recently lamented the state of some of these show-bred terriers and commented that breeders are once again using pedigree fox terrier and lakeland blood in order to 'smarten up' the fell strains, and that this practice is producing non-workers. I can only agree with what he says. Looking at many so-called 'lakelands' at so-called 'working terrier shows', it is obvious that pedigree blood is indeed being used to improve the looks of some of the less 'fine-lined' fell terriers, with not a thought as to what they are doing to working ability. Far from producing sensible, game-working terriers, this practice is producing fiery fighting dogs with little or no hunting instinct and these people, instead of plaguing the working terrier world with their insane practices, should instead invest in Kennel Club registered stock and exhibit at Kennel Club shows where they will do no harm. Most, if not all, the pedigree breeds, including most strains of Bedlingtons and borders have already been ruined for work. The latter are too often bred with chests that are far too large for work, with heads too 'squat' for facing a tough hill fox.

I am not saying that there is anything wrong with trying to improve the looks of a terrier strain in order to make it more pleasing to the eye, or to become more competitive at shows, as long as you breed from good working stock and give the working qualities priority over show points. It is breeding just for looks from non-workers such as pedigree lakelands, fox terriers and Welsh terriers that is the problem. It is true that many of the old fell terrier breeders did this to improve type in their stock, but they lived during a golden age when it was possible to do so without ruining working qualities, for many pedigree terriers were still worked in those days. Many of these improved terriers saw service with most of the fell packs and even the Russells, known as fox terriers then (a different type to the elongated headed dogs of today,) were still worked with hunts, even though they were big show winners, so they could get away with using them in order to produce better lookers. Today, however, hardly any pedigree terriers are worked regularly to their traditional quarry, the fox. So why use them? Always buy or breed from good working stock, for it is the only way to produce the next generation of good, reliable workers, many of which are quiet and get on well with other dogs – an essential quality, especially if they are worked in a pack. If you use pedigree blood you will produce fiery, quarrelsome terriers lacking sense and, equally as important, hunting instinct, and these are useless to the hunting man. Of course, Bedlingtons and borders from good working strains, work well enough and are essential to the continuance of the working qualities

Crag – a looker and sane. A sensible worker. Just the right type to breed from.

A winning border terrier. Borders are used to improve sense, coat type and strength of head on many fell terrier strains.

in these two breeds. A good working border can put sense, coat and head into a fell strain and Bedlingtons, while they are enjoying a great revival as a working terrier, have mainly been used for producing some top-class lurchers.

Having worked your bitch for a couple of seasons and found her a good, game worker, and having settled on a stud dog which is also a proven worker, it is time to go ahead and breed your future stock. It is best to breed puppies infrequently, preferably only when you need young stock in order to keep your pack going, as there are already far too many pups around and too many show-bred pups being passed from pillar to post as their owners get fed up with them and pass them on to someone else. You will often see someone win a few shows with a terrier and then sell it on for a lot of money. It is a vicious circle and one best not entered into, for who wants puppies they have bred ending up living this sort of life? I would rather sell my terriers as family pets than have them suffer the boredom of the show kennel and the hell of several different owners.

Of course, as I have said, it is possible to breed terriers that are good lookers while still retaining their hunting instinct, and quite a few breeders have accomplished this balance, breeders such as Wendy Pinkney of the Pennine Foxhounds, Arthur Nixon (who has produced at least one Great Yorkshire Show winner which was also a legend at work, Sam, owned, worked and exhibited by Tim Poxton), Eddie Chapman and Ken Gould. Many of their terriers really are superb lookers as well as workers. So by all means strive to be competitive at shows while keeping the working qualities such as good coat, nose and sense to the fore and the show bug in its proper place – second to working ability.

You may prefer to buy in young puppies to bring on and enter to the life of a working terrier and there is absolutely nothing wrong with doing this. I have bought in quite a few young pups and have thoroughly enjoyed rearing them and entering them to their work. There is certainly great satisfaction in seeing a young puppy change from a playful novice into a serious, reliable worker, but there is something rather special about breeding a pup yourself and then watching it grow until it at last settles to its work. I would therefore advise that, even if you generally prefer to buy in pups, you breed at least one worker for yourself and experience the joys of rearing and bringing on a terrier you have had from birth onwards.

A bitch usually reaches fertility ten days after bleeding begins, and is best mated any time between the twelfth and the fifteenth day, so, if you will be using a stud belonging to someone else, then make sure that you make arrangements well in advance. At least two matings, say on the twelfth and fourteenth days, are most desirable, to maximise the chances of conception.

Allow a little time for the pair to get acquainted and do not be alarmed if there is a touch of aggression, from the bitch in particular, although if this aggression continues, then it may be best to separate the dogs and try again the next day, for she may not yet be in full breeding condition. If she stands with her tail to the side when the mate reaches her, it is a good sign that she is ready, and she should allow the dog to mount her.

Once he has penetrated and mated her, the pair will tie. It is best to make sure that someone is present throughout the procedure as either dog, or possibly even both, may experience some pain while tied together and fights, especially where fiery terriers are concerned, are not unknown. You may have to help the dog get his back leg over the bitch's back so that they end up tied together while facing opposite directions. The tie can last from as little as a few minutes to as long as an hour, and can be a tedious experience for the onlookers, so a brew and a chat would not go amiss – but always make sure that the pair are not left alone. Repeat the mating at least one more time, a day or two later, although you may prefer three, four, or even more matings; fertility can, in some cases, last up to the seventeenth day. Two matings however, are usually enough.

Once your bitch has been mated, life can carry on as normal for the first few weeks while you wait. If she has been mated during the hunting season, then you can continue working her for the first few weeks – some say up to the seventh week, but I would not work a bitch after the fifth week. I would not recommend mating during the season, however, particularly if they are kept outside in a kennel, as a litter of puppies will be brought into a cold, cruel world during winter, and it will be necessary to use heat lamps to keep them warm. Worse still, your bitch will lose valuable hunting time. If you do continue working your bitch, then be careful which earths you enter her into. If she becomes stuck for a few days in a huge earth while she is pregnant, it is not a good situation for her to be in. It may harm both her and the pups. So be choosy about the type of earth you work with her.

After the fifth week of pregnancy the bitch should begin to show signs of her growing puppies and from then on should be allowed to take things at her own pace (if her walks tire her, then shorten them to suit her). She can be given a little glucose, added to a small dish of slightly watered-down milk, with the chill taken off it with a touch of hot water. Increasing her food intake may also help, but do not give her much more until the seventh week, when another full meal can be given at the opposite end of the day to the normal meal. Of course, if you think she needs more than this, feel free to give it to her – you will soon learn how much extra food she requires.

Your normally exuberant terrier may become a bit quieter as the pregnancy progresses and she may have a sticky vulval discharge throughout, though if this turns to pus, or a greenish black fluid, then it is best to get your vet to check her over. In addition to a little milk after each meal, always provide fresh water so that she can take a drink whenever she feels the need, which could be quite often during the later stages of pregnancy.

It is a good idea to save lots of newspaper, as much as you can get hold of, as this is extremely useful at whelping time and for use as the puppies' bedding. It is very cheap, especially if you get free newspapers through your letterbox, and you could also ask friends and family to save theirs for you. It is easily disposed of when it becomes soiled.

The deeper bottom half of an old suitcase is excellent for use as a whelping box, provided the bitch has room enough to stretch out with her family, or you could use a large cardboard box, provided it is sturdy enough. The sides also need to be low enough to allow the bitch to come and go at will, yet high enough to keep the growing pups contained. Put in a thick layer of newspaper and settle the bitch in at least two weeks before she is due, the date for whelping being sixty-three days after mating took place. Of course, she could be either a little early or a little late, although, if she was mated on both the twelfth and the fourteenth days, and you have counted from the twelfth day, she may not be late at all, for she may have conceived after the mating on the fourteenth day. So check your dates and then recheck them.

In case of difficulties (which are extremely rare), it is wise to notify your vet of when your bitch is due and always make sure you have an emergency number where he can be contacted out of surgery hours, just as a precaution. The bitch will begin tearing at the newspaper and will usually turn round and round, panting and whining a little and possibly vomiting, when whelping is imminent. Just leave her to it, in a warm quiet corner away from any other animals or boisterous children though guard against having the room *too* warm, and keep your eye on her. Terriers are usually eager to please at any other time, but during whelping your bitch will not want to know you, so do not make a fuss of her.

If a pup becomes stuck halfway out, it may be necessary to help the mother by gently easing it out, but if it becomes obvious that a pup is stuck inside her, do not go poking around, as you could do more harm than good. It is far better to call in a vet and let him tackle the job. She may be a little rough with any pups that have already emerged while giving birth to the next one, but do not take them away from her as this will cause her great distress. Check that there are an equal number of afterbirths and pups. You will have to be quick, for she will eat afterbirths. If she retains any of them, she will become sick and a vet must be consulted. Of course, she may take care of the whole business herself during the night and you will be greeted with a litter of newborn puppies in the morning.

After whelping, offer her a drink of warm watered-down milk (pure milk can be a little too rich for a dog) and then, at the first opportunity, clean out the old dirty bedding and replace it with clean newspaper, usually when she goes outside to empty herself, though she may be unwilling to leave her pups for quite a while. But be quick about it, for she will soon be back.

Dewclaws are best left on a working terrier as these help them to get a grip on slippery rocks

At the age of three days, it is time for the pups' tails to be docked and this should legally be done by a qualified veterinary surgeon. Of course, you may be reluctant to have the puppies' tails docked, but be warned; if you leave their tails on, then you may find it impossible to sell them, especially to working homes, for many people are worried that their terriers' tail will get torn badly while working thick cover, or could catch on something while working below ground. The decision is yours, but a terrier with a docked tail is always best.

The dewclaws, however, are a completely different matter. These should be left on, no matter what you read or are told to the contrary. Foxes will hole up almost anywhere and a terrier which works damp drains and slippery rockpiles, in particular, will need its dewclaws to help it climb up the sides of large rocks, which are often wet or worn smooth, or to negotiate drains, where they will help it to get a grip and make its way through the slippery passages.

Ken Roe, who keeps mainly Ward-bred terriers, told me how, while out with the Durham terrier lads, he had seen a terrier get out of a rockpile by lifting itself out with its dewclaws, and he could not stress enough the importance of leaving them on a working terrier, especially those required to work foxes in hilly or mountainous districts. I once watched my own bitch, Mist, climb out of a rockpile up the side of two huge boulders by using her dewclaws to get a grip. The fact that, in twenty years of keeping and working terriers, I have never had to clip these claws on any of them, is, I think, proof enough that they are indeed in use, so leave them on, for it could one day mean the difference between becoming stuck below ground, or getting out of an earth safely.

Once the tails have been docked, all that needs to be done until the pups are due for weaning at around four weeks of age, is to keep the bitch well fed and the whelping box provided with clean bedding on a regular basis. It is also necessary to keep a close eye on the bitch. If at any time she becomes restless and excitable, staggers and lapses into convulsions with rapid breathing, then the chances are she has milk fever and a vet must be called in immediately to treat her with a calcium injection. This is a real emergency, which could result in her death, so be diligent throughout.

At four weeks of age, begin by offering the pups a sloppy meal (cereal with watered-down milk is ideal), and they should soon get the hang of things and begin tucking into this with gusto. As they get older, usually by the age of six weeks, they should be eating three meals a day, one of cereal and two of meat and biscuits. If this diet proves a little too rich for them, then try two of cereal and one of meat and biscuits. This regime can be continued until they are ready to go at the age of eight weeks. Make sure that you provide enough food at each meal time for them to fill up on.

Once the pups begin finding their feet, make sure they are confined and that the bitch can get away from them. You do not want them wandering all over the place, as you could easily stand on one of them, or else you will be constantly chasing around after them in order to clean up their mess. The time your bitch spends away from her growing family will steadily increase until, by the age of eight weeks, she is spending hardly any time at all with them, for she, like you, will by now be a little fed up with them and will be glad to see them go.

At least a month before she was mated, you should have wormed your bitch. It is now time to make sure that the puppies are worm free in time for their departure to what you will hopefully have made sure are good homes. Using a puppy easy-worm syrup, usually chocolate flavoured, puppies can be dosed at two weeks of age and every two weeks from then on. The bitch can also be dosed with the same treatment two weeks after giving birth and again two weeks later when weaning begins.

Looking after your bitch and her puppies well is very important indeed but now all that is left to do is to pick the puppy you will be keeping. Make sure that this one is out of the way when prospective buyers come to look the litter over as someone is bound to want the same one you have chosen and will be disappointed when you tell them it is already spoken for.

Breeding and raising puppies can be a very rewarding experience as long as it is done for the right reasons – to produce the next generation of working terriers. Breeding for commercial reasons is unrealistic, as you may not break even after the costs incurred – stud fee, extra food, worming remedies, vet's costs, food for the pups and the cost of advertising the litter for sale. It will have been worth it in the end though, when your youngster has entered and become a useful member of your hunting team out in the field.

Mother and daughter, Pep and Judy (top of hole), two Jack Russells keenly marking a rat hole.

8

Terriers in the Field

This chapter relates some true accounts of hunting with terriers.

When I went out to the car one day in early December to put my terriers in their boxes, the sun was shining brightly and a gentle breeze was blowing. But climbing out of the car after we had driven into the hills where I was to meet John Hill with his brace of teckels, a biting north wind blew from across the high moorland at the other side of the broad plain below.

I have two terrier boxes, a single and a double, and I would not be without them. They are excellent for keeping terriers contained, which means much less distraction while you are driving, and they also help keep the car clean. Putting them in a box also means that you can stop off at a pub after hunting and enjoy a well-earned bowl of hot soup and a pint, without the worry of the dogs getting mud all over the car, or possibly chewing the seat covers in frustration. I also find that, if they have got soaking wet while out hunting, after a quick rub down with an old towel they will keep nice and warm in their boxes and will soon dry off, provided there is a generous layer of old newspaper and an old blanket for them to settle down on. This protects them from chilling badly, something that could cause serious illness if left unchecked.

A double terrier box; they are very handy for use while travelling; cut down on distractions while driving and, layered with newspaper and an old blanket, keep a terrier warm and dry. They also cut out the risk of fighting.

We drew our first covert, mainly brambles mixed with a little gorse, and, unusually, the pack failed to find, though there was a little scent around. We then crossed a large field and headed for the huge gorse coverts at Mr Walsh's where rabbits abounded. I had visited this place towards the end of August one early morning and had been amazed at the hordes of rabbits I saw feeding out on the open fields and around the shelter of the gorse, and the damage they were doing to the farmer's pasture had to be seen to be believed. They were not only ruining it with their urine and droppings, but also with scrapings and little dug-outs all over the place, almost everywhere I looked. I vowed then that I would return and carry out some serious rabbit control throughout the autumn months. John and I had been doing just that and we had caught quite a few. We then began finding rabbits going down with the dreaded myxomatosis, so had curtailed our visits a little, hoping that some would be left after this awful disease had taken its toll.

The pack found and flushed a rabbit early after entering the gorse and they hunted it for a while, but it proved to be the only one they found above ground, although there were still quite a few around as the warrens being marked by the hounds and terriers testified. It was unusual to find so many rabbits below ground around these thick gorse coverts, where even the wettest and coldest weather conditions hardly penetrated, but, as we drew further along the steep, gorse-covered hillside, it soon became obvious why. Fox scats littered the ground, some outside warrens where, the foxes had dug out and enlarged them. Every fox for miles around must have journeyed to these coverts for the harvest, for rabbits with myxomatosis are very easy prey and they must have enjoyed a great feast over the last couple of weeks or so. I hoped they had settled in local earths.

I remembered a one-holed earth nearby, just over the hill we were now hunting, which I had found a few years before, and we moved off to check it. Fresh sandy soil and stones lay at the well-used entrance, but, apart from a good strong scent which the dogs took a little time over, there was nobody home.

A colony of rabbits had begun to thrive up on the hills where the wind always seems to blow strong and cold, and we set our sights on a place which was full of thick reed beds, where they sometimes lay out, hoping to evade detection by dog, fox or stoat. We had hunted one from this place a few weeks earlier; the pack had entered a thick reed bed on the edge of the high, heather-clad moor where I had not seen any rabbits for years, and we heard one squeal loudly. It came flying out of cover with Fell close behind, the rest of the pack breaking cover a mere second or two later, all chasing eagerly and one or two speaking as the rabbit crossed the wet ground a few yards ahead of them. Sheep netting stood between the reed beds and the vast open spaces of the wild moor, and its small squares allowed only the rabbit through and so stopped the pack abruptly. We were at last able to get hold of them and lift them over, casting where we last saw the rabbit run. Fatima, a tiny creature who does not look tough enough for the rigours of a hunting life, spoke to the line and all went off across the heather and rough stalks of hill grasses until, at last, they lost the scent by the fence.

We had wondered where on earth that rabbit had gone ever since, but today we found the answer. A large warren had been dug in the top corner of the reed-covered moorland and the dogs marked it eagerly. This was obviously the place where the rabbit had run to that day, making good its escape. Not wanting to kill any more rabbits, since their numbers had already been reduced dramatically, we headed up onto higher ground and looked for hares across the boggy ground where tall reeds grew in a few places, bent by the constant strong winds. Everywhere was the weather-worn heather, looking the worse for wear at this time of the year, and a few field-fares, meadow pipits and snipe were roused from their wind-ridden hideaways, flying off across the rugged ground. Hills surround this moorland and the chill wind blew relentlessly as we searched for a hare's presence, the pack casting expertly as they went.

Just as we reached the other side of the moor, where it began to drop to a narrow brook in the valley bottom, a hare suddenly jumped up out of the heather and I cheered the pack onto it. They all gave chase excitedly until it was out of view, probably within a matter of a few seconds, then put their noses to the ground and went away on a decent scent. The pace was quite gentle because the wind was making the scent drift and so we had more than a couple of checks during the first 200 yards or so. I was just saying to John what a lovely pace this was at which to see hounds and terriers at their work when Mist took the lead and went away, going at a cracking speed on what was a screaming scent. John and I now had to run in order to keep in touch with them. This was not easy at all, especially when they crossed a peat bog, forcing us to use clumps of grass, heather and reeds as stepping stones.

One or two minor checks gave us a chance to catch up, but, in the main, they all went well until we reached the other side of the hill, where they swung to the right and struggled a little to follow the scent across the grass-covered ground, which was much drier than

John Hill with fell terriers belonging to myself at a meet with the Holcombe Hunt.

the moor top had been. However, with Fell, Fatima, Fairy and Mist all having a go at casting for scent again and taking turns at leading, they just about managed to fathom it and we knew they were correct and true when we saw the hare rise again about 70 yards ahead. She then passed the trig point and went away speedily out of sight. The dogs struggled again at the trig point and then eventually lost the scent completely.

It was time for me to make a cast and at first I thought I had got it wrong; then Fell took off with all the others joining him, heading off towards the area where it had all started. John and I were a little the worse for wear by this time, but we knew that a rest was a long way off when Fairy picked up the line again, after a slight check, swinging to the left and going at a good pace towards the north-eastern end of the moor, with all four pack members following the scent well until it began to fizzle out as they tried to figure out the line through thick reed beds, along the side of an old, crumbling drystone wall and finally to a narrow track which farmers use to cross the moor. There they at last lost it altogether.

It had been a cracking hunt, fast-paced and extremely exciting, and had lasted for just over half an hour. We worked out that we had covered around 1½–2 miles, for this moor is very wide and long and we had crossed it twice and had then covered nearly the whole length of it. One thing is for sure, John and I had shed a few pounds crossing that moor top like madmen in pursuit of the fleeing pack!

On the way down from the high moorland where the wind had become much stronger as the day drew on, we checked a couple of rockpiles and here Fell and Mist marked a fox to ground. Fell was entered and he bayed like thunder for some time, unable to get up to his fox, which was in a tight spot under a huge mound of rocks. I knew from experience that it was a waste of time to spend too long

Fell, bred by Wendy Pinkney, served for two seasons with the Pennine Foxhounds and is used to working big rough spots like this one.

here, for foxes will not usually bolt when they have a good vantage point where a terrier cannot go. Nevertheless, I gave him time to see if he could manage to work up to it or persuade it to bolt. I did not want to start digging, as I had no mark and would have been digging blindly. Anyway, there were some very large rocks that would have taken some shifting, and then probably only with a machine, so I waited while Fell attempted to make a successful bid for his fox. After a while, though, it became obvious, as it had done on previous occasions at this place, that the fox, possibly one of that year's youngsters which would be able to squeeze into some impossibly narrow places where a terrier could not hope to follow, was not going to budge. When Fell came out a little later in search of another way in, therefore, I grabbed him and John and I moved off, heading now for a well-earned rest, a bowl of hot soup and a cold pint of bitter at the inn where we had met, reminiscing about a cracking day's hunting amongst the wild, vast open spaces of the high, wind-plagued moorlands.

I put on my walking boots and perched myself on the top of Loughrigg Fell long before the hounds began hunting across the silent, darkened woodland at Nanny-Brow. Mist clung to Loughrigg's slopes and rose slowly, silently over the fell top,

Tarn. A Middleton bred terrier who once bolted five foxes from a rock earth in Yorkshire.

Maintaining my sleek, finely tuned figure. Fell hunting can be very strenuous for hounds, terriers and the followers themselves.

shrouding a few followers I could see on top of the crags scattered about, hoping for a quick glimpse of the fox as he took to flight from the Coniston pack. Tarn and Ghyll, my two fell terriers, pulled eagerly at their couples and began to scan the fellside, barren and ice-clad after a long, hard winter and a severe cold spell. They had already heard the blast of the horn and the excited hounds as they began their day's hunting long before the haunting sound had reached my ears.

A little later, a few leading hounds appeared, running through the woodland directly below, and then more and more climbed up the fellside and emerged through a gap in an ancient stone wall, a few keen young hounds baying with excitement and attempting to keep up with the more experienced pack members, magnificent beasts who know these fells and the foxes' hiding places inside out. An engraving shows hounds leaving Ambleside during the early 1800s, so the Coniston pack has been in existence for nigh on 200 years, breeding that helps them hunt even in our day. Young Mike Nicholson, who had taken over from Stan Mattinson at the beginning of the 1996/7 season, appeared through the trees and was soon 'up with' his hounds.

I lost touch with the hounds here, but I soon heard those left behind baying in the kennels at Greenbank, perched on the fellside opposite Loughrigg. They told of the hounds having raised their fox and hunting it through thick woodland above Ambleside village, the home of the Coniston pack. On the fell top I met up with Steve Dawes, the terrierman for the Coniston who has also judged terrier classes at one of the shows I run, and the topic soon turned to terriers and hunting in general. It was while we were talking that a report came over the CB radio of an unadventurous fox that had been run to earth in a crag above Rydal Water, so we hurried to the spot and there, sure enough, were hounds waiting as a terrier worked its fox below ground, attempting to bolt it for the impatient pack. Mike Nicholson's black fell terrier could be heard hard at his fox deep inside the twisted mass of granite boulders, baying like thunder, nipping and teasing, trying all the while to push it out of its lair and back onto the open fell. But it proved to be to no avail. That fox had squeezed into a very tight spot between solid slabs of rock and it was unwilling to budge from such a commanding position. So the services of the terriermen were called upon and the black dog extracted after a large amount of rock had been dug out and then another tried. Still, the fox stood his ground and defied all attempts to dislodge him.

The huntsman therefore decided it would be best to move the hounds on and try for another, asking that the fox be dug out and dispatched humanely, according to law. I was impressed that out on the fells, where laws could easily be broken undetected, these fell hunters stuck rigidly to the requirements. Some hoped the fox would bolt and run another day, but fox control had to be given priority and so excavations continued in earnest, with other terriers dusted by the fox in the process.

In fell hunting, because most earths are huge and virtually un-diggable, if a fox bosses* his opponent (which is often the case, for foxes are accomplished fighters and defend themselves extremely well), another is then tried either to flush it out or to finish

* Dominates, gets the better of.

it underground, for foxes left for another day often worry lambs another day. This is when the follower has a chance of one of his own terriers being used for, when all the hunt servants' terriers have done their bit, they then look to a follower to provide back-up. Ghyll is a Breay/Buck* type bred through John Parkes' lines and is a very strong terrier. The hunt servants thought him more than capable of tackling this fox, which was rapidly becoming a legend as there was much talk of a huge dog fox that was more than a match for the average terrier. So I was asked to try Ghyll after Steve Dawes' rough fell dog had been extracted.

The hounds had by this time found again and we could hear their haunting cries echoing amongst the fells around Grasmere. Our efforts were stepped up, for baying hounds are enough to draw any man from any task, and at last Steve's dog was reached – and with it the fox. So Ghyll remained on his couples that day, deeply disappointed. With bated breath, we all awaited our first sighting of the 'huge dog fox' that had put up such a valiant fight. Instead, the sight which greeted us was of a very small vixen, one of the skinniest little things I have ever seen. We were astounded and just could not believe that this fox could have stood its ground for so long against such game terriers. But it had and it is true that small vixens in a commanding position are among the hardest opponents a hunt terrier will ever have to face.

Steve quickly despatched it with the hunt pistol and a good fox met its end, an end that could not possibly have been more humane. One bullet, not even a blink or the slightest flinch, and it was over. After many years of studying and observing foxes in all aspects of their lives, including being hunted, I cannot come up with a more humane way of controlling these cunning, gutsy predators than with hounds and terriers.

In the early eighties I was busy hunting a bobbery pack**, as mixed a bunch as one could wish for – terriers, mainly Russells with a couple of fell terriers, lurchers and the odd greyhound or two. At one time one of the famous Westmeade greyhounds was a member of our pack, with which we hunted for rats, rabbits, hares and foxes, often with considerable success.

* The type bred by Cyril Breay and Frank Buck; muscular, slape-coated terriers that are extremely game.
** A mixed bunch of dogs of different breeds and types, lacking uniformity.

Steve Dawes; terrier man for the Coniston Foxhounds with his team of fell terriers (Boxing Day Meet, 2000).

One early spring day, as the season's end rapidly approached, we were out, as usual, at dawn and began hunting along the banks of the River Irwell for rats, rabbits and foxes. This river had been a great otter-hunting stronghold during the golden days of the renowned Bury Hunt, but had since suffered from neglect and pollution, as a consequence of which the otters had long since gone, the fish had died, the charming kingfishers shunned its banks and the rats had moved in in their hordes. This is where our little team came into its own. They had served a long apprenticeship on the rat-infested banks of the River Roche and had now become a very efficient unit indeed, with terriers, lurchers and greyhounds marking holes by the dozen, waiting patiently while the ferret worked below ground and trembling with their ears pricked up, then pouncing suddenly upon their quarry as the rats made for the safety of the deep river.

We had killed many rats on the undergrowth-covered banks of the Roche and had reduced their numbers dramatically, not to mention far more humanely and effectively than any poisons, and we now sought more fruitful hunting grounds. At one particular spot we bolted a large rat from a tangle of exposed tree roots covered in debris and Merle, my lurcher, jumped into the water in a rather vain attempt to catch it. He was a very poor swimmer indeed and, sure enough, as always happened, his back end sank like a heavy stone and he paddled at the water frantically without getting anywhere, just managing to keep himself afloat. I gave a few desperate shouts of encouragement (I had jumped into the icy water once before in order to rescue him and was more than a little reluctant to do it again) and, thankfully, he slowly made progress until he was back in shallow water, where he climbed out onto the dry bank and shook himself vigorously, a little dejected after the rat's easy escape.

We moved on downriver and checked out a nice little piece of ground behind an old factory, which was neglected and overgrown and looked as though it might hold a fox or two. The terriers bolted a couple of rabbits from cover, which were quickly taken by Merle and Bess, but no foxes had settled there that day. Rats were rather scarce on the river for some reason – maybe someone else had hunted this stretch recently – so we moved away to some old railway lines and did some ferreting until we came to an old yard where a large bulldozer had begun work shifting ton after ton of rubbish in an attempt to clean the place up a little and level some ground. A commotion there captured our attention and we soon set off to investigate, our curiosity growing by the second. The bulldozer was making very slow progress indeed and it was not long before we discovered the reason. With every few inches the machine moved forward, hordes of rats exploded from the rubbish heap and swarmed all over the yard, some being crushed to death by the bulldozer while others were caught and quickly dealt with by the dogs,

Merle, Pep and Rock, central figures of our pack in the eighties.

which went into action immediately, slaying rat after rat, twisting and turning and dodging all over the place until all the rats had either been accounted for or had escaped. The machine then moved forward a few inches more and the action began again, with dozens of rats milling about around our feet in an attempt to escape from the pack. Some succeeded, but others died from a swift blow from a thin stick I had picked up, mainly for fear of one of them getting up my trouser leg!

This exciting action went on for some time and many rats were killed, mainly by the dogs, which got stuck in with gusto until the machine driver clocked off at last, leaving us no choice but to head for home. We did a count and 101 rats had perished at the hands of our little pack, while many more remained crushed to death in the rubbish heap, unable to get away from the deadly edge of the steel bucket in time. It had been a good day, one that left us all weary with exhaustion, and the pack members with the added burden of sore and fast-swelling faces from rat bites.

Once home, I treated the dog's wounds with warm salt water (I use this treatment three times a day for both rat and fox bites) and then got them bedded down for the rest of the day. I then went round to the house of a friend, Chris, with whom I had done quite

Rock and Pep checking a man-made rock pile in an old quarry.

a bit of digging. While I was there, another friend called in to say that his terrier was trapped to ground in an old quarry and asked if we could help.

I took Rock and Pep along, their faces sore and swollen a little, and Chris took his fell terrier, Zak. Rock, an old veteran over sixteen years old now, was a youngster then and was just learning her trade, so though she searched the rock earth, she failed to find. Pep, though an excellent little fox dog with which I had enjoyed many a long dig, was a little weak when it came to working very deep rock holes and so she too failed to find, for this earth was very deep indeed. It was Zak, a son of Arthur Nixon's Sam through Tim Poxton's border bitch, Mocky, which finally succeeded in the end, dealing with the fox quickly as he always did, but emerging without the little black bitch, Crags, which had entered several hours earlier. She never was found and one can only guess at her fate. She was a small bitch with a small head and could have been outgunned by the fox, or she may have fallen into a crevice and been unable to get out. It is impossible to say.

This had been a long, hard day for all of us and well illustrates how game and hardy terriers can be. After a hard day's ratting which left them weary with exhaustion, my brace of terriers still went to ground and did their best to find in that earth. This is just one of the reasons why I admire working terriers so much.

Ted Robinson's farmland is a mixture of small woodlands, gentle rolling pastures and steep hills criss-crossed with ancient stone walls which climb high and give out onto open heather moorland. It is a glorious place in the height of summer, when a cooling breeze always blows over the flowering heather, accompanying the song of the larks, but a desolate, wind-plagued wasteland during the iron grip of winter, which feels the relentless cold even when the lower ground is enjoying mild conditions. It is a place where I go to hear the wild call of a lonely curlew, to see the thrilling sight of a falcon on the wing, and to follow the hardy moorland foxes which thrive in this area, mainly in the sanctuary of a large, unsightly quarry where rabbits abound, forsaking the earth for rock fissures cracked open by the constant blasting.

Sheep tread and fox tracks twist and turn across this lonely place, remote still despite the hustle and bustle of nearby towns, and, when the snow is down, usually long before it settles in the lower dales, I often track foxes and never fail to be surprised at some of the distances they cover.

Partridges often burst from cover, roused by the busy laal* terriers as they expertly cast for scent across the ground, and fly off rapidly across the broad, sweeping moorland which seems to go on for ever as one ascends its gentler contours until, at last, one begins the long descent down the other side. Hares, too, crouch into the hardened hill grasses, weatherbeaten and stunted, and the tough stalks of the heather which grows profusely up on the higher ground, erupting as the dogs come upon them and racing off with their long ears erect, their longer legs driving them across the uneven surface at incredible speeds. The terriers follow eagerly, yapping furiously when the hare is in sight and, when it is out of view, hunting keenly with their noses to the ground. They will not catch a hare, but hunting them helps a young terrier to use its nose, an essential quality when it comes to finding foxes in huge earths and thick, well-established coverts.

Ted had lost over thirty lambs to fox predation during the spring, and he could stand it no longer. He called us in after we had offered our services, desperate to stop the onslaught. Tim and I, informed of the presence of badgers, searched for a sett and finally found it,

* 'Small' or 'little' in fell parlance.

Fell in the snow.   *Mist in the snow.*

a huge place deep inside a rocky labyrinth at the edge of the quarry. Now we knew which area to avoid, Rock and Bella began their search for the foxes.

We found a litter of well-grown cubs in a small, ancient quarry. Six or seven lamb carcasses lay rotting around a huge rockpile where we attempted to catch them. It was an impossible place; the cubs simply went deeper where it was undiggable, always out of reach of the terriers as they climbed into narrow fissures hardly big enough to allow even a rabbit access. They therefore had to be left after hours of hard work. At least the vixen had moved them well away from Ted's land, which was one consolation. We found another litter, again deep inside a rockpile, and these were duly dealt with while two adults were shot on the lamp a couple of nights later, after a lot of exhausting terrier and lurcher work. Tim had a son of Brian Plummer's Merle at the time, bred by and purchased from David Hancock, and like his famous sire, he was an incredible fox dog, hunting them from cover and marking to ground as well as a reliable old foxhound.

We had ended the previous season well into May, once the predation had stopped, and had promised the shepherd that we would be back during the next season, when we would do our best to cull the large number of foxes whose main stronghold was in the quarry nearby.

Fell terriers doing what they were bred for; working the big rock earths that foxes seem to favour

When September came round again, we parked on the lane above the farmstead at the end of a long, narrow wood and headed into its cool shelter as the sun beamed down out of a blue sky, relieved only by a few drifting white clouds. I only had Rock out that day (she was usually all that was needed) and she put her nose down, ignoring the obviously unoccupied earths on the hillside before entering a massive patch of thick undergrowth, a mixture of willowherbs, nettles and brambles whose fruits would soon be ripe enough for picking, a good place to find a fox, especially on a warm day such as this.

We heard her speak somewhere deep within cover and she began working towards us where we stood silently at the edge of the wood. The covert was behind some old farm buildings where at long last the fox emerged, only a few feet from where I stood. It turned sharply to the right when it saw me and raced off, with Rock not far behind, through the farmyard, under a heavy metal gate and across a broad field, heading for yet more woodland. The ground was bone dry and held little scent, so Rock was soon back with us and followed eagerly as we set off in pursuit, hoping it had gone to ground somewhere ahead.

On the way, we came across a large barn full of hay and my bitch marked eagerly at a narrow space between two bales, eventually squeezing inside and working her way through the passages, keen to catch up with her fox. She pushed herself on and climbed up and over the bulky bales, making her way steadily to the back of the barn, where it soon became obvious that she was in trouble. We made our way round and found that she had fallen down a gap in the hay bales as she attempted to climb towards the fox, and could not get out of the tight space where she was held. Tim went back to the farm and soon returned with a spade. The back wall of the barn was made up of steel panels and we had to dig down through the hard ground and under the panel until, at last, we were able to clear enough space to allow the terrier to squeeze through and come out into the welcome fresh air. The heat must have been stifling in there, the air stale, filled with the strong, musty scent of the fox, which had climbed high up amongst the hay bales. We felt it was too risky to allow the terrier another go, so we decided that this time we would have to accept defeat.

Gerald, a local smallholder who kept mainly hens, ducks and geese, had shot sixteen foxes during the late autumn and early winter of one season. He had struggled against the odds to keep his little place going and foxes had taken a heavy toll on his livestock, so one could not blame him for dealing with the problem in this way, although I could not help feeling that shooting every fox in the neighbourhood was perhaps a little drastic, especially since this area had provided me with plenty of work for my terriers in the past and I feared that there would not be any left if he carried on the way he was going. I promised to look round to see if any more foxes were around.

Snow had fallen heavily during the past few days. I thought it was a perfect time to check Gerald's place, as the heavy cover would have been flattened, making the approach to the earths much easier, and a spot of tracking would hopefully be possible.

I parked by the side of a lake and admired the glorious views surrounding me, especially the snow-covered hills towering into a stormy sky. Rock was with me that day and as we set off along the shore I was pleased to see a healthy bird population out on the icy water. Half a dozen cormorants sat on a long jetty, trying to keep their balance as the freezing wind threatened to blow them off their perch. Goosander and greylag geese drifted silently on the water, sharing it with mute swans, and tufted and mallard ducks.

A crag earth full of fox scent, but lacking in foxes themselves.

Rock sniffed at the entrance to the old drain by the side of a railway line which had long since been abandoned, and walked away uninterested, a sure sign that it was unoccupied, despite looking lived in. I then set off for the place I called Heron Valley, confident that if a fox was going to be found today then that was where it was likely to be found, for blank days had been few and far between there. Indeed, Rock marked eagerly at the first earth I tried in this narrow valley, but the lack of prints at the earth's entrance seemed to contradict her. I loosed her from the couples and she soon disappeared into the darkness. Her baying and digging confirmed the accuracy of her marking which was never really in doubt, for she was by now far too experienced to give a false mark. The snow had stopped in the early hours, so the fox must have been in there for some time, as its prints were now totally covered over.

It was not long before Rock had dug on to her fox and she soon settled down at what must have been a stop end in a one-holed dug-out rabbit warren, an earth I knew well, for I had dug out and accounted for a fox on a similar snow-covered winter's day during the previous season from this very earth. I was certain that Rock was not going to allow her fox to go anywhere and so I started to dig down to her, not at a very great depth, but with a tangled mass of bramble roots and heaps of rubble and ash to contend with, I knew it was going to be hard going.

It took over two hours of hard work, some of the worst moments being the ones that I spent trying to chop my way through thick roots which seemed like lumps of rubber, my spade simply bounced off them. But at last I broke through to my bitch, who worked with added zeal now that her master had reached her. I cleared all the debris from around the hole and in no time at all a fox looked out at me, cautiously, but without the hysterical fear that sentimentalists would have us believe they feel. Now came the dilemma: should I despatch this little vixen in fine winter condition who had handled herself with courage throughout the proceedings, taking Gerald yet another prize, or should I let her go to run another day, hoping she would leave the farmer's stock alone? Finally, I pulled my reliable, hardworking bitch away from the hole, stepped back a couple of paces and allowed the little vixen to emerge from her lair. Off she went in a hurry, through the thick tangle of undergrowth which hung low to the ground, burdened down with a generous layer of snow, with Rock now in hot pursuit – in vain, of course, but as a reward for a hard day's work well done.

I felt that taking sixteen foxes in the same area during the last few weeks was enough. The livestock thefts had stopped, and Gerald had not been troubled since, so culling was not exactly urgent. Moreover, breeding time had come round again and this was a healthy vixen which could breed cubs to help repopulate the area. I had already culled fox numbers in the area myself too, so I felt that releasing that fox to run again was fully justified, for I hate to kill a fox unless it is absolutely necessary.

Fox control should never involve wiping out every fox one comes across. Lamb killers and poultry stealers must be hunted and despatched, true, but sometimes it is best to allow your fox to live, especially in an area where the population has been decimated.

Dan Russell, in his interesting book, *Jack Russell and His Terriers*, mentions that many tales were told of the sagacity and almost human reasoning powers of Russell's dogs and I think there is a very good reason for this. Of course one must allow for some exaggeration, as most tales grow a little 'taller' over time, but I think Russell's terriers do seem to have displayed a great deal of intelligence, and I believe the manner in which they were worked has a lot to do with it.

Without busy roads, or ramblers who might pick up a dog they think is lost, not to mention badger laws, Russell and his contemporaries were able to run their earth dogs loose with the pack and these little tykes, in an effort to keep up with hounds or find them, especially when they had gone away on a screaming scent, would need to use brains as well as brawn. Moreover, Russell spent a great deal of time with his terriers, often allowing them into the house, and hunted with them on a regular basis, thus giving them plenty of opportunity to develop their intelligence. I have already described the incredible antics of Tip, a terrier which worked several seasons for Parson Russell (see chapter 2). This time I want to focus on another of Russell's terriers, Nelson, who obviously had a superb nose and more than a little intelligence.

Nelson was so named because he had lost an eye in a fight with a cat (now there's a good reason for breaking your terrier to cats!) and he had a reputation for being a stranger to fear. Hounds had run a fox to ground near Tetcott and the earth proved to be huge, with a honeycomb of passages, one underneath the other, where the terriers just could not find their fox at all. These earths can be a nightmare for a terrier to negotiate and I remember Wendy Pinkney of the Pennine Foxhounds telling me about such a place, a very large old stone drain near Hawes in the heart of the Wensleydale Foxhounds country, where hounds had marked a fox to ground. This drain has passages going off in all directions, with double drains in places, and she entered Mist, a very promising young terrier which, after a little time, eventually found her foxes – three of them in fact – and bolted them to hounds, which succeeded in securing all three of them. Nelson must have been made of similar stuff, for he emerged from the earth and began digging eagerly. Russell had obviously learned to trust this terrier implicitly, for he confidently announced that he would forfeit his head if the fox was not under that very spot. Nelson did not let him down, for he went back into the earth and began baying furiously. The fox was finally dug out and released for the hounds to resume the hunt. I dare say that any terrierman or woman today would be more than proud to own a terrier which was capable of such feats.

I first saw Crag at Gary Middleton's kennels when my wife and I were staying at his farm one cold January while hunting with the Coniston Foxhounds, and I was very impressed with this neat little red dog, a descendant of Sid Wilkinson's superb dog, Rock. A little later in the season Gary was due to travel down from the

Which way did they go? Looking for hound or fox on the fell.

Lakes for a day out amongst the Lancashire hills where I have permission on several sheep farms. Unable to get that little dog out of my head, I asked Gary to let me have him and he promised to bring him down the following Saturday.

Gary had not actually seen the dog at work, so he could not guarantee his ability underground, but on the first day he acquitted himself well, so I was pretty sure that he would settle to his vocation without too many problems. A day out on the steep slopes of Ballycombe Crag later confirmed this.

It was a warm, sunny day early in the season. The first tints of autumn were showing and a slight chill in a soft breeze heralded the approach of another winter. Ghyll and Crag – whose original name, Greg, I had immediately changed – were put on their leads while Rock ran loose amongst the deep heather and loose scree and rock piled up on the fellside, lest a fox be passed unnoticed. After watching Rock hunting the line of a fox she had just roused, the full length of the hillside, Gary described her as a pack of hounds rolled into one, and, sure enough, her superb nose came into play once again as I watched her follow a strong scent across a scree-bed at the foot of the fell and then up through the heather, still purple after a glorious August display, around rockpiles and then up to the top at Ballycombe Crag, where she disappeared. The fox lay somewhere in one of several passages which wind their way through this large rocky outcrop. A little owl flew from its cold stone perch, skirted the fellside and landed on an old stone wall in the valley below, indignant at us for disturbing its rest.

I thought the day was far too warm for a fox to be to ground, so I was pleasantly surprised when I heard Rock begin baying amongst the rocks, telling me that she had at long last caught up with her fox. She then fell silent as it attempted to confuse her and shake her off by running around the chilled stone passages in order to fill the earth with scent.

When this happens, terriers will often emerge to look for another way into the earth where they may have a better chance of finding their foe, which is why they must be given a little time to settle to the job, and this is what Rock now did. Taking advantage of the opportunity, I managed to grab hold of her before she had a chance to re-enter the earth, coupled her to Ghyll and then released Crag, who soon went to ground once he had tasted the Fox's fresh, tantalising scent. I had no idea how he would fare in such a large earth, but a red flash shooting from the earth soon allayed any fears that this place might be beyond him. I released Rock and Ghyll as Crag emerged on the line of his fox and all three terriers now headed off to the top of the crag and hunted its line across the open moor where they eventually lost it amongst the peat bogs where scent quickly faded in the warm sunshine. Still, I could not complain. Most of my hunting here had been in gale-force winds, rainstorms and fierce snow blizzards, sometimes waiting hours for a fox to bolt from this crag, so it was a pleasant change to have it warm and sunny for once, although I was pretty certain that only one fox would be daft enough to be to ground on such a day.

When hunting a fox they have just bolted from either a covert or an earth, I always encourage my terriers enthusiastically and give them lots of praise, making a fuss of them when they return. They love this, for it is their reward for a job well done when they are unable to taste the carcass. I made a huge fuss of all of them after they had returned to me, then we moved on to try elsewhere.

Rock entered a large gorse patch lower down the fell, not 50 yards from Ballycombe crag, and almost immediately marked an earth

Crag in kennels, a good worker, but not the most intelligent of dogs. I once dug him out of a stone drain because he failed to figure out the need to backtrack. A Middleton bred terrier.

before disappearing below ground once again. I forced my way through the thick tangle of undergrowth and soon came upon a dug-out rabbit hole where Rock was baying strongly. Ghyll was around fourteen months at this time, a good age to begin entering most terriers to fox, but I feared that he was not yet ready for a dig, as he was still very immature and a little oversensitive. Maybe a bad fox bite would put him off his work underground in the future. I could not risk giving him a too tough a task at this stage of his entering, so I boxed him and then headed back onto the fell with Crag and the necessary digging tools.

When I returned to the earth, Rock had dug on a little further and I quickly set about getting a mark on the locator and then began digging down to her. The going was quite good, as the soft soil gave easily and within minutes Rock's hindquarters showed in the hole below and I extracted her a few seconds later and replaced her with Crag immediately, keen to see how he would cope with a dig.

He bayed steadily and strongly and appeared in the hole every time he dodged the rapid lunges of the fox, which waited just around the corner and struck at every possible opportunity which presented itself. I now followed the hole and dug above Crag, with great care to avoid injuring him, and soon had him uncovered and the fine broad-headed fox in a tight spot at the end of the tunnel. He was a magnificent specimen and his coat and brush were in superb condition for the time of year. Crag had given a good account of himself against such a valiant foe and had proved his worth as a working terrier.

Crag showed that he was not a hard dog, as many of the Middleton-bred terriers are, but a better dog to dig to you could not find, for he bayed continually and stayed with his fox until I reached him. I also did rather well with him in the showring, though he was a little too small for many judges – those that did not recognise that smaller terriers of around 13 in (33 cm) are actually favoured by fell pack huntsmen.

Crag was a little on the small side, it is true, but he had a good strong head and a superb iron-hard jacket that was more than a match for our winter weather. However, he just would not settle in kennels, even though he was a kennel dog. Sadly, I was therefore forced to part with him as I already had two terriers in the house, one of them a dog. I had many good digs with him and he also bolted quite a lot of foxes for me too.

Entering a terrier to quarry is mainly a question of common sense, based on a knowledge of its character. While certain guidelines are necessary for entering to certain quarry – rats and foxes in particular – it is no use having hard and fast rules on the right age for introducing them to the animals they are required to work. Like human beings, they are all individuals and what suits one may not suit another.

Patience is essential and the people who allow their dogs to progress at their own pace are the ones who have the most success – that means not giving up on the individual who goes to ground and bays for only a few minutes before emerging again. Do not be disheartened, for many legendary workers had such inauspicious beginnings. As I have said, it is very important that a terrier is not pushed in any way during the entering process. I know of one 'terrierman' who allowed his three-month-old dog to go to ground on a fox, where it bayed at its quarry. Fortunately, he recovered it before it could be mauled and thus be ruined forever. A bad mauling at an early age can have one of two effects. Either the dog will refuse to look at a fox again, or it will become too hard and receive a bad drubbing every time it goes to ground. It is wisest to hold back an

A quiet word of encouragement is enough when putting a terrier to ground. (Merle and Rock.)

early starter until it is mature enough to cope with an irritated fox without being overwhelmed by the situation, and to be patient with a slow starter.

As we have seen, rats can bite pretty savagely and more sensitive terriers should be held back a little from tackling them; while most terriers may be ready to tackle them by the age of around eight months, sensitive ones will undoubtedly benefit from being given another couple of months or so to mature, thus ensuring that they are not put off their work in any way. Another thing to be wary of during the course of a youngster's entering programme is not encouraging it too much when putting it to ground. A few quiet words are more than enough at such a time; too much 'geeing up' can eventually cause the dreaded false marking syndrome that can ruin a terrier for good. This is a problem rarely mentioned in terrier books, but it is one I came across a few years ago.

I was invited to join a couple of lads for a day out in the hills, where many foxes can be found skulking in rocky dens, dug-out rabbit holes, or maybe an ancient stone drain. Rock was steadily progressing in her entering and had joined in quite keenly during a hard five-hour dig a few days earlier. Pep had quite a bit of

Pep and Rock check an old mine working, a likely place to find foxes.

experience at working foxes and that is why I had been asked to come along, for Paul had just bought a new dog, Grip, a big, rough-haired fell type which had more than a hint of bull terrier about it, and Pep was along in order to find a fox for him to try.

It was a bitterly cold day and an icy wind swept down the valley from the bleak hills above, which were never friendly, even during the summer months when the sun blazed across the brown, barren moorland. We tried many earths, but none held, though a find looked ever more probable as we approached a freshly dug earth in a remote little valley which separated Egerton Moor from Hound Tor, two steep hills where I have enjoyed many a fine hunt over the years. I encouraged Pep to try the well-used entrance and she did not need to be asked again. She eagerly approached it and carefully tested the scent around the rough edges and then checked the stale air inside. Satisfied that she knew all of the answers, she then walked away, totally uninterested. She had already proved herself a reliable marker of earths and I had no reason to doubt her – that is until Grip pulled his owner over to the earth, where he sniffed and snorted and then dug at the sandy soil, keen to get below ground.

Paul released him and he soon disappeared, his booming voice coming from around 7 or 8 ft (2–2.5 m) inside. Disappointed and more than a little embarrassed because of my terrier's sudden tendency to false mark, I helped with the digging and we soon reached Grip, who continued to bay furiously as we cleared a space around him so that we could see what was going on up front. We peered intently into the gloom of the musty earth and, as we cleared enough of a space to be able to see in front of the dog, I smiled to myself. What Grip was making all the fuss about was a large stone jutting out of the soil at the end of the tunnel. So it was he, and not Pep, which was the false marker. I have to say that I was relieved that Pep had proved true once again, though I did feel sorry for Paul, who looked rather down in the mouth when he discovered that the earth was indeed unoccupied. It was not his fault, nor that of the dog. The fault lay with Grip's previous owner, who had forced the dog to go to ground and had constantly yelled encouragement at him even when the earths were empty, and thus eventually taught him to false mark in an effort to please his master.

This is a terrible fault which no terrierman wants in a working dog, and it is easily avoided by allowing a terrier to develop at its own pace. If it does not want to go to ground after you have given a little encouragement, then leave it alone until it does. If a terrier is bred right, it will eventually begin going to ground and searching the dark, narrow passages below. If your terrier ever does develop a tendency to false mark, then only allow it to go to ground in occupied earths that have been marked by an experienced terrier, and keep doing this for a few months until it has gained enough experience to know what is, and what is not, an occupied earth. This may cure this bad fault, but there are no guarantees.

A lot has been written about the steady decline in the working abilities of the border terrier over the past couple of decades or so, with some people believing that most will work if entered properly as long as a great deal of patience and gentle handling is applied. Some people believe that most are very slow at entering, no matter how they are treated, while others say that they will often enter early but can remain a little unsteady and unreliable until they mature, for many borders remain puppy-like long after other breeds such as the Jack Russell and the fell terrier have matured and settled down to their work. One of my fell terriers which has a great deal of border terrier in her make-up, entered early, but she was a little unsteady until she at last settled down at around four years of age. A friend's border terrier was a very slow starter indeed, so I guess there is an element of truth in all the theories put forward.

A brace of borders. A lot of borders can be a little slow at starting their careers.

Most terriermen require a terrier to be a made worker by the age of two, so a lot of borders just do not suit them, hence their decline in popularity recently. Added to this is the rise in popularity of Russell and fell types as show dogs, with few borders winning championships at working terrier shows, while many unworked strains make it very difficult to get the right working blood in a puppy. The result is a recipe for disaster.

All is not lost, however, and the following story shows what can be accomplished if a little patience and perseverence is applied.

Tim first saw Mocky in the kennels of a friend of his and he liked her immediately. He asked if she was for sale, but the answer was no. However, a week later he received a phone call and a deal was struck. The reason for this change of heart will soon come clear. At this time Tim had in his kennels Sam and Bella, two Jack Russells bred, reared and entered by Arthur Nixon. Both of them were incredible workers who had seen service with three different hunts with Tim, and at the Pennine Foxhounds with Arthur. Tim had also won the Great Yorkshire Show with Sam, along with many other big championships during the eighties. So it is not surprising that, with this superb team at his disposal, he quickly set about entering his new dog.

He had been extremely keen to purchase this bitch, but his enthusiasm began to diminish when, after several digs over a period of around two seasons, Mocky refused to enter and would not go to ground, though she would work rats eagerly all day long. This is probably the reason why many borders and terriers with a great deal of border blood in their pedigree are written off as failures. Tim decided that, if she refused to enter during the very next outing, then she would have to go, for a working dog must earn its keep.

At an earth located high up in the bleak Lancashire hills, where the wind rages wild enough to blow a strong man over, Sam entered and soon found, baying strongly. It was then that Tim noticed his bitch showing some interest in the proceedings. After letting the excitement build for a few minutes, he released her from the confinement of her couples and, to his delight, she flew to ground at last and stayed to her quarry for the next three hours, which was not at all bad for her first dig. From then on she never looked back.

By the time Mocky had at last entered, Tim had obtained the post of terrierman to a northern pack of hounds, a post he held for three seasons, so it was not long before he had a chance to try his bitch again. The pack were hunting their home ground near to the kennels and a fox was soon found skulking in the heather not far from Herne Crag. Instead of turning his nose for Redghyll Crag, an undiggable fortress that is death to any unwary terrier, he set his muzzle straight ahead and set off across rocky ground and through deep, springy heather on the side of the steep fell. Tim had a good vantage point and watched as the fox made his way unhurriedly towards a woodland which clings precariously to the hillside, a place full of bracken which provides excellent cover to a hunted fox, always keeping a good distance between himself and the pursuing hounds.

The pack pressed him hard in the wood, and he soon emerged at the other end, then made his way across the moor and finally disappeared into a deep rockpile at an ancient quarry that has stood barren and unused for a very long time. Tim was soon at the spot and it was not long before the hounds and the hunting field arrived too. The huntsman stationed his hounds nearby while Tim slipped in a terrier, hoping to bolt the fox. Now pretty sure of her abilities, he chose to enter Mocky, which disappeared inside the earth with fire aplenty, following her fox deep underground. For twenty minutes or so there was silence, the only sound coming from a lonely curlew far out on the windswept moor, but then, somewhere towards the bottom of the quarry face, Mocky could be heard baying like thunder. A few minutes later, the fox bolted from the dark passages at great speed, with Mocky close behind, almost on its brush.

Although this fox then made good his escape by heading across the road just outside the little elevated village and crossing land forbidden to the hunt, Tim was more than happy, for his little border bitch had at last settled down to her work and he now felt that the rewards far outweighed the inconvenience of having to wait for her to accept her true vocation in life. So give a dog a chance, give it time to catch on, persevere. The rewards are well worth it.

I sat huddled in front of a roaring open fire with a hot cup of tea gently cradled in the palm of my hands, comfortable and content as the wind howled outside, often thrusting great clusters of large hailstones against the panes, sometimes disturbing the terriers which lay snoozing in front of the fire. A knock at the door rudely interrupted my lazy afternoon and I answered reluctantly, to be greeted by a good friend of mine, Dave, who crouched in the doorway in rather a vain attempt to shelter from the bitter elements.

He came in from the cold street and told me that he and Paul, another good friend of mine, had been rabbiting at Ballycombe Crag where one of Paul's terriers, Bramble, a rather leggy Jack Russell with more than a hint of whippet about it, had entered a rock earth and had begun barking relentlessly. Being rabbit hunters in the main, they wanted me to take my experienced terriers along to see

Rock and Pep.

if she was onto a fox. I was more than a little reluctant to leave my haven of comfort and warmth, but I soon warmed to the task ahead as I loaded the terriers into the van. I was keen for my little team to see a bit more work while the season remained with us, for it would soon be over. Pep was by this time a veteran at working foxes, but Rock was only eight months, so she would remain coupled while gaining valuable experience listening to Pep at her work.

We pulled up on the flat ground outside the remote farmhouse and quickly headed out onto the fell where we began to climb to the large, craggy outcrop above where we could just about see Paul waiting patiently by the earth's entrance. The rain and hail had relented for now, but it was difficult climbing through the deep tangle of heather and over the loose scree with the wind buffeting and pushing and pulling us every which way. However, it was not long before we had reached the crag.

I then set about getting organised. Bramble had never seen a fox before, but it was obvious from her constant baying that a fox was indeed at home, though her inexperience showed when she returned to the entrance, a little baffled because of the unfamiliar creature below which stirred hidden instincts from deep within her. We netted up as best we could and I released Pep from her couples and entered her. She found her fox almost immediately. Her bay was strong and sure in the dark passage between the slabs of solid rock, formidable and unmoveable.

Bramble joined in, a little more confident now that she had reinforcements, and we waited outside, growing ever more apprehensive as dark, burdened clouds tumbled across the grey sky towards us, where they eventually let loose a torrent of heavy rain with hail, sleet and even a little snow thrown in for good measure. We were soaked to the skin and chilled to the very bone, shivering uncontrollably outside while the battle raged inside, the fox standing its ground stubbornly.

At one point we heard some movement below and I moved just as the fox popped its head out of one of the bolt holes. It undoubtedly saw me, but I think it was probably the net that stopped it making a dash for open country. Instead, it turned, made its way even deeper into the rock fissure and stayed there. Despite the fact that Pep used all her experience, her irritatingly loud, yappy bark, nipping and teasing in good Jack Russell fashion, it simply would not move. All her efforts were to no avail in the end, though she carried on trying while we froze for hours on end, helpless as the dark winter weather threw its all at us.

Bramble soon tired of this strange game and emerged, but Pep carried on regardless, for she was a stayer and had remained with her fox for upwards of twelve hours on some of our longer digs. It was very difficult indeed trying to tempt her away from the job she loved to do. Eventually, however, I managed to call her out as there was not a chance of shifting that fox from what it knew to be a strong, impenetrable fortress

I was absolutely wet through and colder than I had ever been before, or since, and it took a hot bath, hot tea and plenty of time in front of a roaring coal fire before the last chill had been chased from my body.

Foxes will often remain in an earth that proves to be a strong fortress such as the one at Ballycombe Crag, especially when the terrier stands off its fox, baying and teasing rather than closing with it. I have encountered this sort of thing in several places, especially in the Lake District, where foxes often flee to a fortress earth whenever they are roused by one of the fell packs. I have seen foxes make good their escape on several occasions at the Kirkstone quarry and the old quarry at Elterwater, places where they are safe from the attentions of the Coniston Hunt terriers.

While fox-hunting with hounds and terriers is most certainly an effective and humane method of controlling fox numbers, it has to be said that the odds are stacked in the fox's favour where they have this type of earth for use as a sanctuary. A fox in such a place, as long as it is patient and wise, is usually safe from all attempts to shift it, unless of course a hard but sensible fell terrier is entered which knows how to finish his fox underground without taking a mauling. It is not surprising that, with the Lakes riddled with fortress earths, this type of terrier was valued highly amongst the old fell hunters in particular.

Early one January, snow fell quite heavily and lay in frozen white streaks up on the high hills of Lancashire, where strong winds had piled it up in long drifts behind stone walls and around remote rocky places. It was bitterly cold up there and I watched as Ghyll followed a strong scent up the steep hillside towards High Crags, where he eagerly checked the large black rockpiles for the scent of a fox.

A huge bracken bed covers the hillside below this crag, and during the autumn Ghyll had found a fox lurking below the thick mantle of green ferns which were just beginning to turn to rusty red as the winter approached. He had pushed it up and over High

Rock and Bella.
Fell terriers of a
type to be found in
the Lakes for the
past couple of
hundred years.

Crags, across the reedy hill above with reed beds scattered every-where, before it had turned again for the bracken bed and led Ghyll a merry dance. At last he had worked out its line and followed it to where it was hiding amongst the twisted masses of rocks. Forcing it out, he had then hunted its line across the face of the crag and then into cover once again where it had at long last managed to shake him off its line by running around the dark passages of the thick undergrowth and filling them with scent, thus confusing him.

Today, however, High Crags failed to hold and Ghyll dropped down off the rocks at the southern end and hunted through a large reed bed, where a fox had obviously been recently, for he followed its scent keenly. We checked the earths and gorse coverts on Egerton Moor, but all to no avail. Most of the cover had been flattened after the recent snowfall and the icy blast of gale-force winds.

We walked back up the valley to a good spot, which often holds a fox or two. An old drain here has held foxes on more than one occasion and I was hopeful of finding again today. As I headed along the ancient track which once led to the many old mills which flourished here many decades ago, making my way to the drain which had been so fruitful before. Ghyll headed off to my left and stopped at another old drain, which runs the whole length of the top of a small hill. I had checked this pipe many times in the past and had never known it hold even a rabbit, let alone a fox, so I was rather surprised when he began marking the entrance.

It was a little too tight for Ghyll, who was a trifle too large in the chest, so I took him to the other end of the drain and he followed reluctantly, not wanting to leave the entrance, where there was obviously a strong scent wafting out to his sensitive nostrils. The wind was blowing strong and cold right up the valley and it blew straight up the pipe. Because of this, there was no scent at the other end, and Ghyll refused to enter, returning rapidly to the first entrance where he dug eagerly, trying to squeeze into the partially blocked hole.

This is just one long pipe and I was sure that a fox would have bolted by now, owing to all the noise we had made, so I dragged him away, convinced that a rabbit, a rat or maybe a mink was holed up in a tight offshoot of the pipe. I dragged him away to the earth I

Ghyll – Show Champion and a first class worker.

was keen to try, but he showed no interest at all and ran off, back to the old pipe, where he began to mark once more.

For eleven seasons I had relied mainly on my old fell bitch Rock. She always marked true and could find in the deepest of earths. There was also Pep, a Jack Russell whom I suspect had a little Plummer terrier blood in her make-up, Bella, a daughter of Rock sired by Chris Rainford's incredible working fell dog, Snap, and there were Crag and Tarn, two smart-looking terriers from Gary Middleton's strain of fell terrier. Tarn once bolted five foxes from a rock earth in Yorkshire, and Ghyll had provided back-up over the years, but Rock was the one I trusted implicitly. I was forced to retire her but she had such abilities that I used her for another season while in retirement, adding another twenty foxes to her already substantial tally. I now had to learn to put my trust in another terrier.

Time and time again, Ghyll had proven his worth as a worker, but I now failed him, for I did not heed what he was telling me. As I was walking away from this place, attempting to get Ghyll away from the pipe, he ran along the hilltop, possibly realising that this was his last chance, and flew up the pipe, baying strongly and bolting a large fox, which shot out of the old pipe and ran across the ground, which was strewn with piles of old stone from the mill ruins, crossed a swollen beck which carried away the melting snows, and finally went out of sight.

Ghyll emerged soon after and hunted its scent across the rough ground for a while, but failed to find his fox again. I had absolutely no chance of netting the end of that pipe and it was all my fault. I had failed to put my trust in a terrier which had earned it – a mistake I determined not to repeat.

We are all still learning, no matter how long we have been working terriers and, I suppose, nobody, no matter how experienced they are, will ever 'know it all'. If there is just one thing that is certain and predictable about this game, it has to be the unpredictability of the fox and a day spent hunting him.

High up in the cold hills above Accrington in Lancashire, along a narrow, rough farm track which winds its way up the steep hillside to the bleak dwelling above, is a small tip, only a few square yards in area, which was literally full to bursting with rats. Many years ago a few of us would get together at the weekend or during the holiday period and we would hunt our little bobbery pack on rabbit, hare, fox and rats. We had a great deal of ratting permission back

Bess, Merle and Rock, integral members of our bobbery pack during the 1980s.

then, mainly picked up from local farms where Roy, one of the group, worked pretty regularly, repairing tractors and other farm machinery. We also had some cracking spots along riverbanks and small litter-ridden brooks where the rats thrived in the dirty, polluted environment. It was while Roy was repairing some farm machinery that he was told about this small tip and its resident rats. He immediately told me about it and a day was set for our little team to pay it a visit.

I had many ferrets at this time, but I always took my best two on ratting expeditions. Jick, a polecat ferret, was the best that I ever worked, though coming a close second was Numbhead, so called because it seemed to take her an age to catch on to her true vocation in life. However, she became the fastest worker I ever saw in action once the penny had at last dropped and she had entered to her work. She was able to clear large warrens – even those in rock – and rat holes in no time at all.

We headed up the long, winding track that took us deep into the heart of the Lancashire moors and soon pulled up at our new hunting grounds. We were rather disappointed at first because of

Jick and Numbhead, excellent working ferrets. They flushed many rats and rabbits for our pack.

its size, or lack of it, and we began to feel that we may have wasted both our time and our money. However, when we inspected the place and the dogs had had a chance to look around, keenly marking every hole they came to, we began to feel a little more optimistic. Roy had brought along his two terriers, Bonnie and Judy, two excellent working Jack Russells, and I had brought Rock, Pep, Merle and Bess, two terriers, a lurcher and a greyhound, all of which were by now seasoned ratters.

This place is very bleak indeed; only tough hill grasses will grow, bent and twisted by the constant winds that howl across the exposed moorlands, tormenting the hardy sheep and the tough hill cattle which mainly fend for themselves amidst a harsh, infertile landscape where the few trees that do grow are stunted and twisted by the hostile weather. Any dogs which stray a little too close to these cattle soon find out how wild they really are. It was the unlikeliest place to find a large colony of rats, but it turned out to be a rat catcher's paradise.

Jick and Numbhead were released from their sack and quickly made their way into the dark, narrow tunnels that twisted and turned through and around the mounds of stinking rubbish which had been so thoughtlessly dumped there. It was not long before the first of the rats began to make for open country. The dogs, of course, were eagerly awaiting their emergence and they quickly snatched up the bolting rodents one after another until the two ferrets reappeared, having evicted all the tenants from those particular lairs. However, not all had been accounted for. A few had managed to evade capture and had disappeared into the darkness of other holes,

Jick, an exceptionally good ratting ferret.

so the two ferrets were simply left to their own devices and they quickly found other holes which they entered eagerly, setting about the evictions once more.

The team of dogs swiftly snapped up as many as possible, but a few more did escape and managed to get below ground as before. And that is how things progressed for the rest of the day. Most were accounted for as they bolted, but always one or two got around the awaiting pack and made good their escape by getting below ground again, or by squeezing under some item of rubbish. But Jick and Numbhead got their noses to the ground and soon caught up with them.

One of us would pull up a piece of rubbish or roll away an old steel drum and a skulking rat would be snapped up almost before it could move. At one spot, Jick entered and a little time later reappeared at the entrance, emerging backwards. She dragged a large dead rat out of the hole before quickly re-entering. Then, once again, she emerged from the hole backwards and dragging yet another large dead rat out into the open. She had finished them both by biting through the tops of their skulls – a very quick death indeed.

By the end of the day we were all exhausted and more than ready to go home. It was not a case of the pack just standing around and snatching up fleeing rats as they tried to pass them; it never is. The place was full of obstructions – metal drums, old tyres, scrap metal etc. – of which the rats took full advantage for shelter, so the dogs had to work very hard indeed, bobbing and weaving and stretching themselves to the limit.

We made many trips to this little tip and we took large numbers of rats every time. Then they began to dwindle and at last none could be found. We had done what had been asked of us. We had rid the farmer of a disease-ridden pest, even if it was only a temporary measure. Rats will often return to a place and then it will be time for the dogs and the ferrets to return too, for there is no better way to carry out pest control than with a couple of good ferrets and a bobbery pack, mainly consisting of terriers to catch them as they bolt from their lairs.

I was on a sheep farm deep in the heart of the Lancashire hills where large numbers of foxes have caused havoc over the years, not only with the shepherd's flocks at lambing time, but also with ground-nesting birds, whose numbers had dropped dramatically. The large bracken bed at the foot of Hound Tor did not hold a fox so Ghyll went on ahead of me onto Egerton Moor where he eagerly marked a dug-out rabbit hole. Pushing on into the darkness below, he dug out small sections of the tunnel where it was a little too tight for him to negotiate further. I like a leggy terrier with a good-sized chest to match and do not mind too much the short wait while it makes room to press on deeper underground. True to form, it was not long before Ghyll caught up with his fox and his strong, steady bay boomed directly underneath where I stood. The ground thudded as he cleverly dodged the fox's lightning attack.

When I first began hunting this area a few years ago, I found that there were large numbers of foxes concentrated in certain areas, with one earth I visited holding nine foxes at the same time. In these areas ground-nesting birds were almost non-existent. Hounds hunted here until a short time ago and these concentrated groups of foxes would not have been formed had they still been doing so, so I decided to do what the hunt was no longer able to do, though on a much smaller scale, of course.

For the past few seasons, from September through to March, I have regularly drawn all the coverts and checked all the earths where I have permission to do so, driving out the concentrated groups of foxes, dispersing cubs, killing some and allowing others to run for another day, and I believe that my efforts are working. I have noticed a steady increase in the number of ground-nesting birds during recent years. Partridge and lapwing have returned and are nesting in areas where they have not been seen for years, and the once familiar cry of the skylark comes down from the heights above the green fields again. I was delighted to come across a flock of dunlin at the water's edge in a secluded little valley just recently and there has also been a dramatic increase in the number of wood-cock during recent years. A shooting friend has been carrying out his own fox control programme and he, too, believes these methods are paying off.

It is only possible to disperse these large groups of foxes properly by using hunting dogs. Good, busy hunters who cover every inch of every covert and drive out any foxes that are using it as a refuge. If hunting with dogs is indeed banned, then the consequences will be disastrous. I have seen the damage done where good fox control

A brace of good working terriers are an excellent means of carrying out effective pest control.

is not carried out. The effectiveness of dispersal carried out from late August through to the close of the season should not be under-estimated.

Using a spade, I removed a large square of rough turf and dug down easily through the soft soil. A cold wind blew strong across the boggy high ground, bending the tough hill grasses and chilling me to the bone whenever I stood still, listening to my terrier teasing his quarry in the darkness below ground. I eventually broke through and took a few seconds to clear the break. During this time, Ghyll had typically closed with his fox and throttled it quickly. It was a fully grown dog fox in excellent condition and, though I was saddened at the death of such a fine animal, I knew that it was necessary for a safer, less troublesome lambing and nesting time ahead.

On this particular farm there was no trouble from foxes during that spring, for the first time in years, though the same could not be said of other places. I was called out to a couple of sheep farms that spring and at one place a large dog fox was often seen feeding in the garden on scraps of food left out for the birds. When the farmer's wife's miniature Yorkshire terrier began barking and ran at it from the kitchen, the fox turned on it and chased it back into the house; the farmer's wife arrived just in time to stop the fox's attack. She was convinced it would have killed her dog had she not inter-vened. The fox just ambled off untroubled when she chased it away. Noel, the shooting friend I mentioned earlier, was called out and he shot a large dog fox which may have been the culprit, for that fox has never been seen in the garden since.

Noel and I were called out by another shepherd to deal with a fox that had been seen chasing his sheep at midday. We covered every inch of his ground with terrier and gun, and found some excellent earths that looked well used, but, alas, failed to hold this time, and lambs continued to be taken. After a lot of hard work and miles of walking, we eventually tracked the culprit to a large, inaccessible crag where Noel shot a vixen, which was obviously the guilty party because the troubles stopped there. There is no doubt about it: hunting with dogs is necessary if the countryside is to be managed properly and our farm livestock and ground-nesting birds are to be protected. Ban hunting with dogs and foxes will be poisoned and trapped on a scale never seen before, something which will cause much more harm and suffering, not only to the fox, but also to other wildlife.

9

Mink-hunting with Terriers

Wherever mink are to be found, which is just about everywhere these days, water voles, the beloved 'Ratty' in Kenneth Graham's *The Wind in the Willows*, are fast disappearing, indeed they have become extinct in some areas. Research has shown that pollution is not to blame, nor is loss of habitat, for otters have returned to many water courses, which indicates that the rivers and streams and their habitat must be healthy. The finger of blame points at the mink; they are very efficient predators which just love water vole. They have colonised Britain, partly as a result of a few escapees from fur farms, but mainly because of the unthinking and unreasoning animal rights people who have invaded these farms and have released these incredibly potent killers into the wild, with devastating consequences for our native wildlife.

In an effort to protect our wildlife and farm livestock, (for mink can easily get among hens, ducks or geese and can cause devastation when they do), mink hunts have been set up, using hounds and terriers. The season runs from spring through to the early months of autumn, when the rivers begin to swell and chill again, making further hunting rather more dangerous.

I became interested in mink-hunting after a day out fox-hunting. Gary Middleton and I had spent all morning and part of the afternoon checking all the earths I knew of in a particular valley, but they were empty. Wondering if the weather was still a little too mild for foxes to be going to ground, I let my old fell bitch, Rock, loose from her couples and sent her into the rusty-red bracken which had now died off, but even there, a fruitful place where she once bolted five foxes at one time out of covert, failed to hold. We shrugged our shoulders and carried on, my bitch taking full advantage of her freedom as she put her nose to the ground and cast around and through every bit of cover she came across.

At the bottom end of the valley there is an old stone drain. It is an ideal spot for foxes to use as a den but, after many years of trying it almost every time I hunted that particular area, I had never found it in use despite the obvious wear and tear around the entrance holes which showed that foxes at least visited it. I was rather surprised, therefore when my bitch scraped away a pile of dead leaves and squeezed into the narrow entrance, as keen as mustard as she tested the stale air filled with the musty taint of fox scent. Her loud baying told of success and a fox popped out very quickly indeed, before Gary could reach the earth (he was eager to try one of his young entries, which he was just starting). I could have kicked myself for leaving Rock loose, but at least Gary's terriers could enjoy the fresh fox scent which filled the earth as they eagerly explored it.

Gary loosed them one at a time and each in turn drank in the musty scent which hung heavy in and around the earth, and one of his terriers in particular, a black and tan bitch called Slug (she resembled a slimy slug when she was born), showed a great deal of natural hunting instinct as she searched for her quarry, first below and then above ground. I was most impressed with this bitch and Gary told me that he had had high hopes for her ever since she had found and killed a mink without any previous experience whatsoever.

He had taken his terriers for a walk alongside a little beck which runs through a charming valley near his home in the Lake District, when Slug began marking a hole at a mass of tangled, washed-out tree roots – a likely place to find mink, although of course rats will also frequent such places. Having no digging tools, Gary returned home to collect them. With all the noise he made, digging and geeing up his terriers, the mink eventually bolted into the icy beck and, after a short, strenuous run, was caught and quickly despatched by Slug.

It was after this tale and a few reports of mink sightings that I decided to have a go myself on my local rivers and streams and I have had mixed success, including some excellent, exciting hunting.

My daughter accompanied me to a local stretch of river one day, where my old fell bitch, Rock was put to work. Rosebay willowherbs, nettles, brambles and many other wild plants grow strong along the banks of this river, with a few large stone piles here and there, so there was no shortage of coverts and hiding places for the agile mink if they had chosen to live in this region. I sent my terrier into as much cover as possible and her eagerness to push on in places told of scent left by rat, rabbit, fox, or – hopefully – mink. We waited patiently, hardly daring to breathe, for Rock's loud, sometimes irritating bay, heralding a find, but each time she would emerge from covert without a sound.

We arrived at the final stretch of river to be drawn that day and I noticed my terrier casting about and following a fresh scent along the bank, which was strewn with debris from the river. A tree stood out into the water a little way from the bank and it had a huge stick pile entangled in its branches and a whole host of other debris which had obviously been left behind after the river had swollen with the autumn and winter torrents. Here Rock was at her most eager, barking, tail wagging furiously, scratching keenly at the base of the tree as she marked it for all she was worth. We stood still and watched as she began to climb the tree and to dig her way into the stick pile.

We watched for rats bolting, as this was what I thought she was hunting, but out popped a mink instead, making a bid for the open after the terrier had come a little too close for comfort. It emerged on the river side of the tree and dropped into the cold water, swam a little downstream and then disappeared along the bank, heading south. Rock soon figured things out for herself; she quickly made her way down the trunk of the tree and cast around it for scent. She picked up the mink's line and followed it with zeal, finding the spot where it had emerged from the water and going rapidly away until the scent began to fade in the hot sunshine. She could not fathom its line any longer, and eventually lost it. I was pleased, though, for we had enjoyed a find, a flush and a good, exciting hunt on our very first outing; not bad at all. We tried a few more places, but without success, despite coming across mink prints and quite fresh kills, though we did find another mink a couple of weeks later.

It was difficult for my bitch working these long stretches of river alone, so I borrowed Judy from Gary Middleton's kennels and used her alongside Rock. We were working a particularly difficult stretch of river when Rock picked up a scent and the pair followed it downstream. It led them through thick, tangled bracken thickets, over stone piles, where I hoped for a mark, to a large outcrop of rocks by the river's edge, where we found the remains of fresh kills under a bridge and up a steep bank. They both began marking a few holes which led under some huge blocks of solid stone. They tried to squeeze into these small tunnels, keen to get at the musky scent below, but all to no avail. I got stuck in myself and had a good go at bolting the mink, making as much noise as I possibly could and doing my utmost to make inroads into this lair. It proved to be a real stronghold, however, for, despite our best efforts, we failed to shift that mink and were forced to leave it for another day.

I have enjoyed limited success while out mink-hunting, and have come to learn that the two most important things are perseverance and terriers with good noses. Mink can be found in a variety of places: amongst most types of undergrowth such as willowherbs, brambles, nettles, long grasses, reeds and rushes. Debris left in riverside bushes and trees is always worth checking, and also any stone piles, where mink will lie up for the day after having taken over a system of rat holes. Rats can pose a bit of a problem while looking for mink as a terrier will usually hunt them readily, even if they have not been previously entered to them.

I well remember one mink hunt with Rock, Ghyll and Crag which was one of the best and most exciting hunts I have ever witnessed. Muffled whimpering and furious tail-wagging heralded a find in a very large and particularly thick covert – a mixture of bracken, brambles, nettles and reed beds. The three terriers worked keenly and extremely well, eventually working out the difficult line (summer hunting is often much more difficult due to drier conditions), and soon caught up with their quarry. They then went on to hunt it for what seemed like an age up and down a narrow brook which runs through quite a deep gully, covering quite a long distance as they went. I failed to get a view of the quarry, but surmised that it was a mink, for I was sure that a rat could not have covered the distance or run for that length of time. However, as the pack made their way back towards me, I spotted an extremely large, fat rat in the brook below and this time it broke cover and got out rapidly, for the dogs were close on its tail and would have accounted for it had it not got out when it did. The pack followed its line for a while, but finally lost it after a good, long hunt. So if you wish to hunt mink seriously, or wish to work for a mink hunting pack, then it is best to break your terriers to rat so that they do not become distracted while hunting mink.

A little common sense is needed too, when working terriers in water. Our weather seems to be becoming wetter and as a result our waterways are swollen on a more regular basis, something which calls for caution. If rivers are dangerously swollen, then obviously hunting along their banks is very risky, as a terrier could easily be swept away. It is best to keep away at such times, for even a strong man can come to grief in a rapidly flowing river.

There is some controversy about which breed of terrier is best suited to mink-hunting. Personally, I do not think it matters, though a bit of leg on a terrier will certainly help it to negotiate the many obstacles encountered while hunting such terrain. Having said that, border terriers always excelled at otter hunting and are no doubt very useful for hunting mink, as borders love water and have excellent jackets which easily shed cold water after a dip in a river or stream. Most terriers will take to mink-hunting.

Though they are only small creatures, mink can bite with great ferocity, so it is not wise to enter a terrier to mink until it is of an age when it can cope with such quarry. If it is less than ten months, I do not believe it is ready to face a mink, especially as a terrier after a mink in water can be bitten quite severely.

Mink-hunting helps a terrier to use its nose and this will come in useful when it begins its work to foxes a little later on, helping it to find and to learn the art of marking an earth as occupied. Hunting mink will also help it to grow in confidence and will aid the natural entering process.

10

Places to Avoid

Having your terrier stuck fast below ground is not very pleasant, to say the least, although it is an experience that most terriermen will go through at some time or other, especially when hunting foxes regularly. There are, however, things that can be done to lessen the risk of your terrier being trapped in an earth. Of course, the terrain being hunted has much to do with the degree of risk and some places, such as the Lake District, are notorious for bad earths and for the numbers of terriers trapped in them.

Some hunt countries contain deep and difficult rock earths which are best avoided, even if they are marked as occupied either by the hounds or the terriers themselves. Other places are pitted with old mineshafts and these can be deadly places for a terrier trying to find and flush a fox. Deep sandy earths are typical of some hunt countries and can be just as deadly as rock earths or old mineworkings, for the sand can fall behind a terrier which is pushing onto its fox in a tight place and can block off not only its exit but also its air supply, with obvious consequences. Some places, including the hilly districts of Lancashire which are my main hunting grounds, contain all the above types of earth and more, and it can be a nightmare trying to hunt foxes, in such places. Happily, I have not yet lost a terrier to ground even though my team of workers cover a vast area, with many bad earths of all kinds, and they have been trapped on several occasions. I have learned a lot over the past couple of decades and now take great care when putting a terrier to ground, although it is impossible to be certain of the outcome every time a terrier enters an earth, whatever the type.

Old, disused quarries are a favourite haunt of foxes and can be very fruitful hunting grounds if you have good, reliable finders in your team, as these types of earth can be extremely deep and the highest quality finding ability is needed if you are to hunt them successfully. I would avoid the actual quarry face at all times as cracks in the rock, usually as a result of continuous blasting, can be

Terriers'-eye view of fell hunting country. (From Ivy Crag, Loughrigg Fell.)

extremely deep and are often pitfalls for unwary terriers. If they fall into these narrow crevices they can remain there for ever, for digging such places is usually impossible.

Piles of old stone are ideal places to find a fox and are usually safe enough to work as they are simply man-made heaps of stone – unlike borran earths, which are a natural part of the landscape and can be very dangerous places to work, for they are often extremely deep and are usually undiggable where passages run under huge granite slabs of rock which are difficult to break up, even with blasting. Many of these types of earth* are therefore generally best avoided. I know of one such place deep in the heart of the western

---

* Experienced local terriermen, whom you can meet at shows or terrier club meetings, will let you know which earths are best avoided in your area, for many, such as Redbrook Crag in the western Pennines and Broad Howe borran near Troutbeck in Cumbria, have reputations as bad places.

Borrans, like this one, are often found below crags.

Borrans can often be deep, dangerous places and care must be excercised when entering a terrier and whilst digging.

Pennines where it is impossible to rescue a terrier from its depths, and many have been lost for good there. Its fame has spread far and wide in the north of England because of the number of terriers' lives it has claimed. Foxes love these strong fortress earths and you will usually find them occupied; they know they are safe in such lairs.

Old stone drains are another favourite type of earth. They are ideal places for working with a terrier, especially a youngster, for most of them are very straightforward places to negotiate and all the dog has to do to find its fox is simply to run the length of the tunnel. Foxes will readily bolt from such earths which, in the main, are quite easy to dig. However when I revived the Mid-Lancs area of the Fell and Moorland Working Terrier club in 1994, I was called out because a young terrier had got into trouble after being entered into an old stone drain on the hills above Rochdale, a place which is frequently used by foxes. Rock and Crag marked the drain eagerly, but I was more than a little reluctant to enter either of them as there were capped mines in the area and drains, I had been told, could be outlets for flooded shafts. We searched up hill and down dale for the other end and did our utmost to locate the terrier, but without success. Alas, it was never seen again. I advised the owner to call in the fire brigade with sound equipment and to place ads in local shops and newspapers just in case it had got out and had strayed.

During that same week, three terriers out at exercise entered another drain nearby and they too never emerged, probably lost in the old mineshafts that litter the area. (Some old mine workings are fairly safe to work, while others have reputations as deathtraps.) So take great care when entering a terrier into an old stone drain and if you see capped mines in the vicinity, then it may be best to leave well alone. Some old drains also lead under old mill ruins, where a terrier could become lost in the labyrinth of passages which are often to be found under the ruins – though these days, of course, the use of a locator considerably cuts down the risk of losing a terrier in such an earth.

Dug-out rabbit holes are a sure sign of an easy dig in most cases, but again, be careful when putting a terrier to ground in this type of earth. One-holed dug-out rabbit burrows can sometimes lead into badger setts and it would be both illegal and dangerous for your terrier, which could easily become lost in a huge, well-established badger sett. So check out the area around a dug-out rabbit earth and make sure there are no badger setts nearby.

Of course, there is always an element of risk involved when carrying out fox control with terriers, but that risk is very small

A stone drain with running water. Foxes will often use these even though they are wet. Avoid this type of earth during heavy spells of rain, for obvious reasons.

Entering the drain

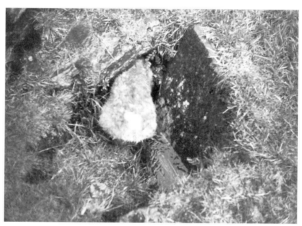

indeed in relation to the number of earths a terrier will enter during an average season. If you follow these few simple guidelines, exercise caution and leave those earths that are too dangerous to try, then you will greatly reduce the risk of getting your terrier trapped below ground.

There are, however, no guarantees, however careful you are and for this reason I strongly advise you to join a recognised terrier club with a rescue service available to its members. The Fell and Moorland Working Terrier Club (F&MWTC) is probably the best, as it runs a nationwide rescue service and will pay the costs if digging equipment or an earth-mover is required. It can also call in assistance from its members if necessary. There are also many

Above: *A fell terrier going to ground. Take care when working drains which can be outlets for flooded mine shafts.*

Left: *Emerging from an earth. This stone drain has held many foxes over the years.*

Merle attempting to follow the terriers to ground in this old mine working.

excellent clubs now operating more locally although funds and assistance may be more limited than those of the national club. There would be nothing wrong with joining both the F&MWTC and a club which covers the local area, as both will provide assistance should your terrier become stuck below ground, and both will put on excellent shows during the summer months where you can get together with fellow enthusiasts and enjoy exhibiting your dogs. Whichever you decide on, the important thing is that you join a club with a rescue service at the top of its agenda, for the sake of your terriers.

It is illegal to disturb a badger sett by entering a terrier into the tunnels and these places must therefore be strictly avoided. While many terriermen dug and treated badgers humanely, often removing them from land where the farmer wanted them either culled or released elsewhere (for badgers can and do take livestock such as chickens and even lambs), others have treated these lovely creatures in extremely cruel ways, ensuring that all who own terriers are now regarded with suspicion. This is a very sad situation, for true badger digging was carried out in a way that caused no harm to the badgers during the actual dig, just a little irritation from a noisy, yapping terrier, followed by a very quick death, humanely administered – or, more often than not, released else-where where the landowner had no objections, often in long-disused setts. The thugs who allow two, and usually many more, dogs to attack a live badger, are very few and far between and should be dealt with severely by the courts, but it is a great injustice to put all terriermen in the same league. Most have great respect for the quarry they hunt and will always do their utmost to finish it as quickly and as humanely as possible.

When you gain permission on farmland it is always best to walk over your new hunting grounds, particularly if you run your terriers loose and hunt cover with them, so as to locate any badger setts which your terriers may encounter. This is best done in midwinter when cover is flattened and sparse and any setts are much more easily located. It is well worth the effort involved and may mean the difference between trouble-free work, and getting into trouble because your terrier has gone to ground in a badger sett you did not know existed. You will receive little sympathy when you try to explain that you did not know of any setts in the area, so be diligent and save yourself much grief. The following guidelines may help you to avoid badger setts.

- Badger setts usually have two or more entrances which are quite large, larger than entrances to fox earths.
- They have large mounds of soil or sand around the entrance holes.
- Grass and other forms of bedding such as dead bracken can often be seen around the entrance holes and trails of it lead into the sett, often with broad paw prints with five toes that leave claw marks. A fox's pad is narrow with four toes.
- Entrances to badger setts are always clean and are free of any remains of prey, unlike some fox earths, especially in spring, which smell musty and have the remains of prey scattered around outside.
- Well-worn narrow paths lead from the sett to latrines and favourite hunting grounds.
- Scratches may be found on rocks or trees nearby or around the sett.

If you have any reason to believe that a hole is a badger sett rather than a fox earth, then leave it and try elsewhere. Occasionally, a badger may use a fox earth as a temporary measure and some people have come upon one when digging to what they genuinely thought was a fox. If this happens, it is always important to get your terrier out as quickly as possible and then leave that earth well alone for a few weeks. Go back and check it and if it has not been taken over by badgers, then it is safe to work once more. It is likely that the badger, having been disturbed while resting in a fox earth after being caught out in the daylight when he had strayed a little too far, quickly vacated it and made his way to his proper home. Finding a badger stealing a day's rest in a fox earth is not the same as disturbing a badger sett.

11

The Showring

The hunting season generally begins at the end of August and, including spring lambing, when troublesome foxes are hunted out of necessity, runs through to around the middle of May, though much of the hunting has usually finished by mid-April, when the summer off-season begins. This period of inactivity (mink-hunting aside), gives the countryside a rest and the animals a chance to breed and swell their numbers again. It also enables the dogs to enjoy a gentler pace of life for a while, recharging their batteries so to speak.

This rest period, can be rather tedious, but summer shows are a good source of activity that will help relieve the boredom of those non-hunting months. They include classes for all the main working terrier breeds, especially Russells, fells and borders, although, much more can be seen. At the big game fairs and country shows, there are things going on in the main ring throughout the day: fly fishing demonstrations, sheepdog trialling (usually using ducks rather than sheep), lurcher and falconry displays, hound parades and more. There are agricultural shows with rare breeds on show, stone-walling and hedge-laying demonstrations and the opportunity to meet like-minded people.

The judges in terrier classes should have worked and exhibited terriers for many years and thus have the experience to make the best decision. Of course, no matter how good the decisions are, and no matter what the reasons for making them, no judge will escape at least a little criticism. You will come across the same complaints at all shows and will soon come to recognise the same bad losers. Having said that, there may sometimes be good reasons for complaint, for some judges can make some amazingly bad decisions. Generally, though, judging is a thankless task and one has to realise that one cannot please everyone. I remember one country show where the same judge had been appointed to oversee the terrier section on both the Saturday and the Sunday, a big mistake

Islay Mist of Holcombe (Midge) owned by Mrs Christine Sneddon.

as it turned out. The same three terriers were picked out on both days in the lakeland dog class and on the first day Crag, my red fell dog, a worker as well as a looker, was awarded second place to one of Wendy Pinkney's terriers. However, on the second day, the same judge gave Crag first place and Wendy's dog second. A judge must have a very good memory if he is to avoid such obvious mistakes! It is always best to have different judges on different days.

Judges should look for a terrier with substance. It should not be built like a bull terrier, but it should have strength of bone and thus should not be as light as a feather when you pick it up. A terrier needs a little weight with it if it is to boss a fox in a commanding position inside an earth. Around 14–18 lb (6–8 kg) is good, especially for a terrier to ground on a tough hill fox who has been driven to earth by hounds. A good jacket that will stand up to bad weather is most desirable, whether smooth or broken, and a judge should be looking particularly for density and hardness, for a soft silky coat is no good to a terrier and will be potentially lethal when working hilly districts during midwinter. Straight legs with narrow shoulders and

Wendy's present team at the Pennine Foxhounds including Vandal and Viper, Nettle and Briar. Fell, the terrier on the end at the far right is now doing some good work at my own kennels.

a spannable chest are also qualities a judge will look for, though I would not rule out a rather broad-chested terrier as long as it was spannable. A good mouth, with the top row of teeth just coming over the bottom row when the mouth is shut is also a good point. Wendy Pinkney, a good judge of a terrier, believes that this type of mouth is the most powerful, for she believes that level teeth weaken the bite. She would rather have an undershot jaw, as this still allows some strength in the bite. A good scissor-bite and large fangs are what she also likes to see.

Big terriers above 14 in (36 cm) at the shoulder at one time did extremely well, but that is no longer the case; most judges now go for terriers of around 13 in (33 cm), give or take a little, although there should be no fixed rule in the matter of size. As long as a terrier is narrow enough at the shoulders to squeeze into a fox hole and is spannable, ensuring that the chest is not too barrel-shaped or too deep to negotiate narrow fissures and tight tunnels, it will usually get to its fox in the end.

A friend of mine was into Jack Russells in a big way and enjoyed considerable success, winning at even the Great Yorkshire Show as well as quite a few other big venues during the eighties with his tidy-looking terrier, Sam. He was a member of the Jack Russell

Fell-bred by Wendy Pinkney, getting a better view of the hounds.

Terrier Club of Great Britain, but became disillusioned with its aims after he had been excluded from the entered class by one judge who told him that his was the best-looking dog at the show, but he was unable to place it because it had a few teeth missing! Terriers will sometimes lose a tooth or two in the line of duty and any judge who fails a dog because of this has not got working qualities in mind and should not be judging working breeds of terrier.

Some terrier shows coincide with the hunting season and there is nothing worse than seeing a terrier at these shows who has fresh fox bites on its muzzle. It is always best to leave an injured terrier at home until its wounds are properly healed, whether working or showing, for it does nothing for the image of fox-hunting, and terrier work in particular, when the public see bitten terriers at shows. There are enough opponents of hunting as it is and terriers with wounds are not a good thing to have on view; people may turn against hunting because of it. Judges too, should be responsible enough not to pick out terriers with fresh bites on their faces and

Fell getting an even better view of hounds.

have the courage to send them out of the ring. Moreover, although a few bites are unavoidable, especially when a fox finds itself in a commanding position, a badly bitten terrier is obviously too hard and lacks the sense of the traditional working terrier to stay out

Ghyll after his successful show debut.

'Rob', Holcombe Jameson. Owned by Christine Sneddon.

'Isla' Hollybridge Isla of Holcombe, owned by Mrs Christine Sneddon.

of trouble and will spend more time laid up injured than actually working.

When preparing your terrier for a show, never cut its jacket, but pluck it out. This ensures that the coat will remain in top condition – in fact, it will improve its condition greatly. Cutting a jacket will only ruin it and will make it soft, lightening the colour and turning a red jacket, for example, blonde. Make sure your dog is not overweight and keep the eyes clean, free of any matter etc.

There are some real characters to be found at shows. I can remember one incident at a show in Ramsbottom in Lancashire. One man had been asked to leave the ring after he had entered his young puppy in the over 23 in (58 cm) class class for lurchers. Deeply offended, he exclaimed as he was leaving the ring, 'He will be over twenty-three inches when he grows up.' His mother, equally offended, stormed over to the ring entries tent and demanded that her son be given his money back. The ring entry fee at that time was only 50p!

Remember never to take showing too seriously and try to accept a judge's decision with good humour. Showing is a means to an end, it is a little activity for the summer months until hunting time

Ch Holcombe Jack Daniels, 'Jack'. Owned by Mrs Christine Sneddon at the Holcombe Hunt Kennels.

'Buffy', Holcombe Hot Toddy. Owned by Mrs Christine Sneddon at the Holcombe Hunt Kennels.

Trophy display for a show I organised.

comes around once again. Of course, there are those who do not work their terriers and are only interested in showing. Each to their own, though I would not buy a terrier from these people because puppies bred from non-workers for just a couple of generations may have seriously diminished hunting instincts and will either be incredibly slow to enter, or they will not be interested in work at all.

These people are very serious about exhibiting and are there to win. It can be interesting watching them at work. If there is good, strong competition in the lakeland class, for example, they will enter their terrier in the crossbred class so as to win a rosette and hope-fully get themselves into the championship at the end of the show. It is very unsporting indeed to put a lakeland type into the cross-bred class where it will usually be unbeatable, and judges should refuse to place a terrier that has so obviously been entered in the wrong class, for crossbred types or fell types are rarely as 'typey' as the box-shaped lakeland and will not usually win where a lakeland is placed in the same class.

Holcombe Jameson (Rob), owned by Mrs Christine Sneddon.

If you decide to go for a Plummer, a Bedlington or a Lucas terrier, there are now several shows which stage classes for these breeds and no doubt the number will continue to increase as they grow in popularity.

12

An A–Z of Terrier Names

I have always been fascinated by the wide variety of terrier names to be found in books or at shows. Settling on a name for a new puppy is far from easy when confronted with so many choices. A great many names evoke memories of days spent out in the field and are apt for our game little workers. Names such as Rock, probably the most popular name for a fell terrier today, are obviously taken from the huge rockpiles and steep, formidable crags of regions such as the Lake District and north Yorkshire, where rock earths abound.

Rock earths are often favoured above other types of earth. Rock is a common northern name for a terrier.

Borrans can cover a vast area.

It often takes a while for terriers to find a fox in a huge borran.

When following hounds across the bleak fell tops of places such as Cumbria, a dense mist will often descend and, until it clears, it is impossible to get the slightest view of the hounds. It is then often best to stay put in order to avoid the possibility of falling over a crag. It is days out on these mist-ridden fells that has inspired the name 'Mist'.

Some terrier owners give names that follow a theme. I can remember when Wendy Pinkney had a team of terriers which she worked with the Wensleydale Foxhounds and their names included Fern, Briar and Sedge – taken from plants which give excellent cover to a fox. I favour names which are associated with the wild places where foxes and other wildlife spend their lives. A name such as Bracken, an excellent covert plant which gives shelter to foxes, suits a red terrier, for bracken turns to rusty red during winter. Crag, Borran (a natural rockpile formation), Beck (a lakeland stream), Tarn, Reed, Moss, Storm and Bramble are other names that evoke memories of these wild, lonely places and make excellent names for working terriers.

Certain names are popular in particular parts of the country; Chanter, for example, has been popular in Northumbria for decades, and probably derives from the melodic part of the Northumbrian pipes. Piper is another name that has been well used in this part of the country.

Naming a terrier is important and I therefore present the following list to assist you in your search for a suitable name for your puppy. There is a wide selection of names that I have collected, or come up with, over the long years that I have been working terriers.

A: Alice (I once knew of a ferret with this name, but it will do for a terrier), Adder (Frank Buck's famous terrier), Ash, Alder.

B: Blen (short for Blencathra, the mountain and fell pack), Bedale, Barley, Boozer (I owned a terrier, Ghyll, a grandson of Tony Broadbent's dog of this name, which was a legendary worker in the north of England), Britt (another legendary worker belonging to Maurice Bell), Bruce, Briar, Brow, Bow, Bess, Bruin, Brunt, Brittle, Bramble, Brock, Breeze, Bonnie, Biddie, Ben, Beano (after Oliver Gill's famous terrier, a looker and a worker), Bantam, Banter, Butcher, Badger, Bink, Blacksmith, Boss, Buster, Brick, Bleak, Blue, Buzz, Bracken (will suit a red terrier), Billy (from Middleton's white fell terrier which has given rise to a dynasty of top winning and working Russell types), Bedlam (more suitable for a hound, but good for a noisy terrier) Borran, Bella (Arthur Nixon's bitch which part-nered Sam) Bingo (Cyril Breay's black terrier which died in an old shaft whilst working a fox), Blitz, Barker (one of the ancestors of the famous Buck/Breay strain of terrier), Beck, Breck (a corruption of Beck), Buffer, Bitters, Brook.

C: Cleeve (a steep valley in Devon), Crag, Crevice, Chain, Cass, Cassy, Candy, Canter, Caffrey, Crab (from Anthony Chapman's terrier which saw much service with the Coniston Foxhounds and carved out quite a name for himself in this area), Clem, Crofter, Champ, Corrie, Cairn, Crest, Coin, Conie (short for Coniston), Crete, Chance, Chancer, Clancy, Cartmel (the village and the fell), Cragsman.

D: Davy (Frank Buck's famous dog which worked as well as he looked and who is the ancestor of most of the black, slape-coated terriers around today), Darky, Dandy, Dusty, Derwent, Dobbin (a terrier which was the sire of many of Johnny Richardson's terriers when he hunted the Blencathra), Doug, Dak, Deadlock (from the famous hound featured in *Tarka the Otter*), Dusky, Dusk, Dusty, Dent, Daz, Dart, Dot, Dobbie, Dick, Devon, Dartmoor, Driver (a place name in Exmoor country), Dell, Dingle.

E: Eskdale, Elsa, Ellie, Exmoor, Eire.

F: Fury (Joe Bowman's dog, a very game terrier) Fern (Wendy Pinkney's bitch which won the Great Yorkshire Show during the early nineties), Forester, Fisher, Fen, Fly, Fell, Fricker, Fritter, Flicker, Flint, Fran, Foxy, Ferodo, Floss, Frisk (from a Cumbrian hunting song), Foiler, Frolic, Fan, Fuss.

Natural hunters.
Fell terriers
scenting heather
in the snow.

G: Gin, Ginnie, Grouse, Grade, Ginger, Gem, Grip, Griff, Growler, Gruff, Gen, Granite, Glen (a valley), Gillert, Gypsy, Galley, Gill, Ghyll (a narrow ravine down a fellside which carries water to the valley floor), Gyp (the famous terrier which saw much service with the Ullswater pack), Gravel.

H: Huntsman, Henry, Heather, Hatty, Hunter, Henchman, Hacksaw, Hem, Honey, Hornet, Hazel.

I: Ike (Albert Benson's terrier which gave rise to the red and black rock strain of fell terrier bred by Walter Parkin and worked with the Lunesdale Foxhounds), Ice, Itsy.

J: Jasper, Jill, Jake, Jenny, Jet, Jed, Judy, Jess, Joe, Jack, Jummy (a terrier which worked with the Coniston pack under George Chapman, a real game dog), Jock, Jimmy, Jim, Jig, Juddy, Jester, Jest, Jelly, Jessy.

K: Kate, Kim, Kipper, Kerry, Keeper (Chris Rainford's border terrier which won well at shows with Bob Atkinson; a harder terrier never drew breath), Kelly (the terrier coupled to the fox in Clapham's book, *Foxhunting on the Lakeland Fells*), Kendal.

L: Lucy, Lucas, Letty, Lentle, Leggy, Line, Lill, Lyne, Lindy, Laddie, Loppy, Ling.

M: Monty, Mantle, Mizzen, Mast, Massey, Morris, Mick (a Blencathra terrier of the Russell type), Mess, Moss, Myrt, Mischief, Meg, Moll, Molly, Malone, Mocky (Tim Poxton's bitch which saw service with the Holcombe Hunt), Murphy, Mint, Mist, Misty, Miller, Maple, Maggie, Mags, Mandy, Miner (an appropriate name for a terrier), Minter, Mona, Moley, Mel (short for Melbreck), Magda, Midge, Mac, Mike, Major, Marshal, Millie, Myrtle, Myrt, Marsh.

N: Nip, Nipper, Nickel, Nidge, Nellie, Newsboy, Ness, Nessy, Nettle, Nelson (Parson Russell's superb terrier which did much work with hounds and had a reputation for fearing nothing), Nectar.

O: Otter, Ox, Oz, Ozzie, Oak.

P: Printer, Pike, Pennine, Penny, Pat, Poker, Pobble, Pedal, Peeler, Preston, Piper, Percy, Pep, Peter Lorre (one of my pups had the same bulging eyes), Pet, Porter, Punch, Pickle, Patch, Prickle.

Q: Queen, Queenie, Quill.

R: Rush, Royal, Rigg, Ranter, Ransom, Rags, Racer, Riff, Ruff, Rift, Renegade, Riss, Ricky, Rocky, Red, Reel, Rebel, Rex, Rydal, Rusty, Rock (after Anthony Barker's famous terrier which worked foxes hard, but with sense, for the Ullswater pack), Rattler, Ruthless, Roy, Rastus, Rufford, Ross (Wendy Pinkney's terrier which saw much service with Frank Buck at the West of Yore and with Wendy at the Wensleydale), Rally, Ridge, Reed, Reef, Ranger.

S: Steel, Spout, Spark, Sparky, Skiffle, Sid, Selwyn, Snap (Chris Rainford's incredible worker which sired my own bitch Bella; the sire of Ghyll also has this name), Snatch, Sally, Scandal, Spiffy, Stream, Snip, Sett, Sherry, Scamp, Shandy, Socks, Sam (after Arthur Nixon's excellent Russell dog which worked with three hunts and won the Great Yorkshire Show in 1983), Storm, Smitty, Smithy, Squeak, Stump, Sheena, Spider, Sedge, Smudge (I knew a good working Russell with this name), Sling, Slinger, Sharp, Sharper, Scree, Slate.

T: Tim, Thwaite, Trim, Timmy, Tess, Tipple, Tuppence, Trencher, Trench, Tweed, Titch, Tickle, Tarn, Tats, Teddy, Trace, Topple, Tinker, Tyson, Tatters, Tanner, Tear 'em (after Joe Wear's famous terrier, which was one of the hardest and gamest ever to work to fox, a terrier with guts and sense to spare), Twist, Tiger, Tig, Tarzan (Johnny Richardson's famous terrier), Trent, Trouble, Teezer, Tip (Parson Russell's terrier, which displayed great intelligence while working), Tex, Taffy, Trilby, Turban, Topsy, Turk (one of the most famous terriers ever to work with a fell pack, he belonged to Harry Hardasty and is the ancestor of most modern fell terriers), Tarquin, Tarka, Tommy, Trixie, Tina, Tony, Tangy, Tartar, Tyrant, Tricksey, Trap, Trimmer, Trinket, Trick, Tack, Twile, Thorn.

U: Ulpha (a lakeland fell), Ulster.

V: Vandal, Vim, Vixen, Venture, Viper (one of Frank Buck's legendary terriers), Vic, Venom, Vicky (one of Dave Harcombe's well-known terriers).

W: Whip, Whin, Woodman, Willow, Wist, Welcome, Wasp, Wendy, Whisky.

Y: York, Yetty.

Z: Zak (a son of Arthur Nixon's Sam and Tim Poxton's Mocky, I worked with this terrier on several occasions and he was a superb fox dog).

Index